ARCO
Typing for Beginners

Prentice Hall
New York • London • Toronto • Sydney • Tokyo • Singapore

An Arco Book

Prentice Hall General Reference
15 Columbus Circle
New York, NY 10023

Copyright © 1960, 1957 by R.B.D. Publishing Co., Inc.
Revised 1968

38 39 40

Manufactured in the United States of America

Colophon is a trademark of Prentice-Hall, Inc.

ARCO and PRENTICE HALL are registered trademarks
of Prentice-Hall, Inc.

Foreword

The typewriter is a machine, and the typist is a human being.

In this book, both are brought together in order that both may learn
to work together.

There was a time, not so long ago, when only business people learned
to type.

In today's world, however, the typewriter has become the familiar
friendly symbol of communication, in the home as well as in the office.
And the typist is anyone who learns to type: student, career girl, business man, professional man, housewife, business woman, professional
woman, etc.

While, in learning to type, no special qualifications or previous train-
ing are required, there are, nevertheless, certain basic skills that must
be learned.

It is these basic skills that Typing For Beginners teaches.

First, of course, the student is introduced to the typewriter and its
mechanical operation. Then, step by step, Typing For Beginners leads
the student toward an understanding of proper typing techniques and
explains their use.

By this means proper typing habits are established and a solid foundation is laid for mastering the typewriter. Every lesson in Typing For
Beginners is a step forward. By the time the last lesson is reached,
student and typewriter should be at ease with each other, doing work
with facility, at an even rate of speed.

Even if the student has had some previous typing experience, it is
suggested that the best way to use Typing For Beginners is to start
from the very beginning. With this book you have a new, easy way of
learning to type.

Table of Contents

Royal

Remington

PARTS OF THE MACHINE

The numbers on the photographs refer to the parts listed alphabetically on the page below.

Parts that are not visible are indicated by underscoring the number.

Smith-Corona

IBM

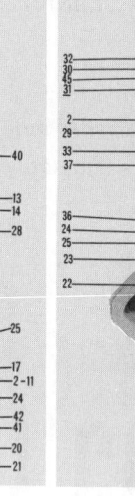

Underwood

Know Your Typewriter

PARTS OF THE MACHINE

28. ALIGNMENT BAR AND SCALE—indicates the line of writing and is a guide for reinserting paper.
24. BACKSPACE KEY—moves carriage backward one space at a time.
9. CARD HOLDERS—metal "fingers" that hold cards, envelopes, or small pieces of paper against the cylinder.
33. CARD HOLDER RELEASE—releases card holders to permit unobstructed view of the typing line.
31. CARRIAGE RELEASE LEVER—LEFT—
13. CARRIAGE RELEASE LEVER—RIGHT—permits moving of carriage to any position.
41. CARRIAGE RETURN KEY—(electric only) spaces lines of typing and returns the carriage automatically to the left margin.
29. CARRIAGE RETURN LEVER—spaces lines of typing and returns carriage to the left margin.
27. COVER—when raised, permits cleaning of keys.
10. CYLINDER—(also called PLATEN) the roller around which the paper turns.
45. CYLINDER KNOB—LEFT—
14. CYLINDER KNOB—RIGHT—used for turning cylinder.
15. CYLINDER SCALE—calibrated to indicate the number of strokes that can be typed across a piece of paper. Also used as a guide to margin settings, tabulating and locating the typing point.
42. ELECTRIC SWITCH AND INDICATOR—(electric only) turns electric typewriters on and off and indicates that machine is on or off.
44. IMPRESSION INDICATOR—(electric only) regulates the pressure with which the key strikes the paper.
35. KEY RELEASE—(Remington only) frees "jammed" keys.
32. LINE SPACE REGULATOR—adjusts carriage lever for single, double, or triple spacing between lines.
18. MARGIN RELEASE KEY—permits typing beyond the margins without changing margin settings.
2. MARGIN SETTING MECHANISM—LEFT—
11. MARGIN SETTING MECHANISM—RIGHT—permits setting of margins.
40. MULTIPLE COPY CONTROL—(electric only) moves cylinder back to permit typing of many carbon copies without cutting through first sheet.
7. PAPER BAIL AND SCALE—holds paper securely against the cylinder. Scale permits check of the typing point.

8. PAPER BAIL ROLLS—rubber rollers on paper bail that hold paper against cylinder.
3. PAPER GUIDE—movable plate that aligns the paper in the desired position for insertion into machine.
4. PAPER GUIDE SCALE—numerical scale that shows where to place the paper guide.
12. PAPER RELEASE LEVER—releases paper for straightening or removal.
5. PAPER TABLE—wide metal piece that supports the paper in the machine.
36. PRESSURE CONTROL—adjusts the tension of the keys.
1. RATCHET RELEASE—(also called LINE FINDER) permits typing either above or below the typing line.
16. RIBBON INDICATOR AND STENCIL LEVER—determines whether key will strike upper or lower half of the ribbon. When placed in stencil position, key will not strike the ribbon.
39. RIBBON RELEASE—(Royal only) permits manual turning of the ribbon spools in either direction.
34. RIBBON REVERSE LEVER—reverses movement of the ribbon.
43. RIBBON REWIND LEVER—winds ribbon onto left spool for changing.
22. SHIFT KEY—LEFT—
20. SHIFT KEY—RIGHT—used to type capitals and characters.
23. SHIFT KEY LOCK—locks shift keys in "capital" (upper case) position. Release by depressing shift key.
21. SPACE BAR—long bar at bottom of keyboard, operated with the right thumb and used for spacing forward.
19. TABULATOR BAR OR KEY—moves carriage to tabulated positions.
25. TABULATOR CLEAR KEY—clears tabulator stops so that new stops may be set.
38. TABULATOR CLEAR, TOTAL—(Smith-Corona only) permits tabulator stops to be cleared without moving carriage.
17. TABULATOR SET KEY—sets tabulator stops.
6. TYPE GUIDE AND INDICATOR—metal slot which aligns key as it strikes paper. The indicator, which is directly below, shows typing point.
37. TYPE INDICATOR—(Underwood only) shows typing point.
30. VARIABLE LINE SPACER—on left cylinder knob. Resets the line of typing.

are quickly sized up by the person who is interviewing you. He   694
glances at you and almost unconsciously forms an opinion. Of   756
course it is your hope that this first impression is a good one.   821
Whether it is favorable or not depends upon whether you have the   886
same idea of what an attractive appearance is that your interviewer   954
has. The first thing he looks for is a neat, tidy, harmoniously-   1021
groomed person. In dressing for your interview, remember you are   1087
going to an office, not to a party, and you should dress accord-   1152
ingly. This generally means simple grooming with coat, dress or   1217
suit, hat, shoes, gloves, all to match. Your hair, of course,   1280
should be neatly set.   1302

The way you walk makes a strong impression upon a person   1359
whose profession it is to interview people. Is your step firm?   1423
Does it show a quiet, easy self-confidence? Do you hold your head   1490
up, your chin up, your shoulders back? Are you relaxed, and do   1554
you have a smile on your face? Is there a minimum of make-up and   1620
yet sufficient to show the good lines of your face? Are the   1681
seams of your stockings straight in the back? Do you feel that   1745
you are making a good impression?   1779

All this an experienced personnel director takes in at one   1838
glance. If the firm you are calling upon is a good one, if it is   1904
a place where you are anxious to work, then remember that the   1966
personnel director is very careful to select only those people who   2033
will fit into this organization. When he talks to you, don't   2095
interrupt him. Let him finish each statement or question and then   2162
answer simply, clearly, and pleasantly.   2202

Keep this in mind if you have made a good first impression: 2262
The interviewer wants you to work in his organization. Almost   2325
unconsciously, he wants to help you secure the position that you   2390
seek. You have won the greater part of the interview with a good   2456
impression. Your good personality has carried over to your   2516
interviewer so that he becomes your friend.   2560

Know Your Typewriter ——CONTINUED

SETTING THE MARGINS

LEFT MARGIN	RIGHT MARGIN

ROYAL

Move left margin control forward. Using right carriage release, move carriage to the desired left-margin position. Press margin control back to original position.

Move right margin control forward. Using left carriage release, move carriage to the desired right-margin position. Press margin control back to original position.

UNDERWOOD

Depress left margin control and move it to the desired left-margin position.

Depress right margin control and move it to the desired right-margin position.

Note: On older models, the right margin control is used to set the left margin and the left margin control is used to set the right margin.

REMINGTON

Depress left margin control and move it to the desired left-margin position.

Depress right margin control and move it to the desired right-margin position.

ON KMC MODEL (Not Illustrated)

Move carriage as far to the left as it will go. Hold down KMC (Keyboard Margin Control) key and bring carriage to the desired left-margin position.

Move carriage as far to the right as it will go. Hold down KMC key and bring the carriage to the desired right-margin position.

SMITH-CORONA

Depress left margin control button. Move carriage to the desired left-margin position and release margin control button.

Depress right margin control button. Move carriage to the desired right-margin position and release the margin control button.

ON OLDER MODELS

Raise margin lever to "left" position and move carriage to the desired left-margin position. Return margin lever to center position.

Depress margin lever to "right" position and move carriage to the desired right-margin position. Return margin lever to center position.

IBM ELECTRIC

Touch carriage return key to locate the present left margin. Depress and hold down margin set key. While holding key down, move carriage to the desired left-margin position. Release set key.

Move carriage to the right until it locks against the present right margin. Depress and hold down margin set key. While holding key down, move carriage to the desired right-margin position. Release set key.

6

tion of the platen is vital and assures a firm grip of the paper — 1847
as it revolves around the cylinder. Be sure to clean the trough — 1912
when you clean the platen. Use a dry, clean cloth to dust it — 1974
out. This prevents the accumulation of dirt and grime in the — 2036
trough and results in finished typing that is always neat and — 2098
clean. Lubricate your typewriter in accordance with careful — 2159
instructions from your service expert. Never oil type bars or — 2222
segments. Remember that too much oil can prove harmful, so heed — 2287
your service expert's advice. Mechanical complications should be — 2353
left entirely to your service expert. Rely upon him for any — 2414
adjustment or repairs other than those simple ones with which you — 2480
are wholly familiar. — 2501

Reprinted by permission of Remington Rand Company.

YOU AND YOUR PERSONALITY

All of us hear so much spoken about our personality. We — 55
have some idea of what is meant by the word, yet few of us would — 121
venture to try to give an exact definition. We all know that a — 185
person is known by his personality. Of course, everyone wants to — 251
have a good, pleasing personality. Everyone wants to be highly — 315
thought of by friends and by all with whom he comes in contact. — 379

You might roughly divide personality into two parts: The — 437
outward one which we call our appearance, and the inner one which — 503
we may call character. Strangers judge you entirely by your — 564
appearance. When you come into an office for the first time, you — 630

(CONTINUED ON NEXT PAGE)

95

Preparing to Type

PARTS OF THE MACHINE

Before typing you must be familiar with the common operative parts of your machine. Study the charts at the front of this book and learn the location and function of each of the following:

PART	NUMBER	PART	NUMBER
Cylinder and Knobs	10, 14, 45	Line Space Regulator	32
Paper Table, Guide and Scale	5, 3, 4	Carriage Release Levers	31, 13
Paper Bail	7	Space Bar	21
Paper Release	12	Margin Setting Mechanism	2, 11
Carriage Return Lever	29	Cylinder Scale	15

INSERTING THE PAPER

Once you are familiar with the parts listed above, you are ready to insert your paper into the typewriter. (Always use more than a single sheet of paper in order to protect the cylinder.)

If your machine is equipped with a "0" mark on the paper guide scale:

1. Set paper guide at "0".
2. Raise paper bail away from the cylinder.
3. Hold the sheets of paper loosely with the left hand and place them on the paper table with the left edge of the paper resting against the paper guide.
4. Twirl the right cylinder knob with the thumb and first two fingers of the right hand.
5. When paper is in the correct position, the left edge will be at "0" on the cylinder scale. (See illustration below.) Then place the paper bail over the paper to hold it firmly against the cylinder.

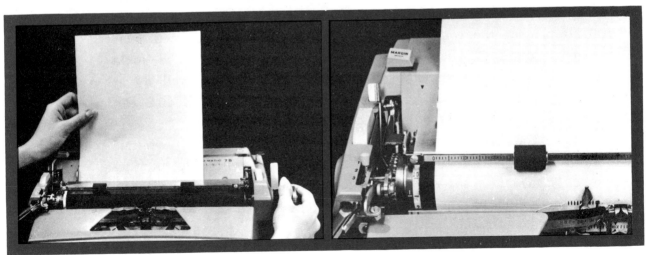

INSERTING THE PAPER   LEFT EDGE AT ZERO

Drill 9

A FEW WAYS TO MAKE YOUR TYPEWRITER
LAST LONGER

Your typewriter needs your daily care. It needs you to take 61
good care of it. It is your office baby. The better care your 125
typewriter gets, the longer it lasts, and the better service it 189
will give you. Your employer will look with favor upon those 251
people who take good care of the company's property. Here is a 315
list of some suggestions which, if conscientiously followed, will 381
earn the smiling approval of your superior: 425

Dust the exterior of your typewriter every morning when you 485
come to work and at the end of the day. Dust is the greatest 547
enemy of the typewriter. Be sure to dust underneath your type- 611
writer every day so that air circulation will not carry dust 672
particles that may lie on your desk into the inner workings of 735
the machine. It is necessary to brush out all erasure particles 800
from the type segment every day. In erasing, remember to move 863
your carriage to the extreme right or left, to prevent erasure 926
dust from dropping into your machine and clogging it. Always 988
brush away from the typewriter. 1020

Release the paper feed rolls during the day when your type- 1080
writer is not in use and always do so at night. This prevents 1143
flat spots from developing on the feed rolls and platen. It is 1207
vital to protect them at this time. Another must is to keep your 1273
typewriter covered when not in use. If the typewriter is in a 1336
dusty spot, place the cover over it during the day as well as at 1401
night. Air circulation is greatest during the day and dirt can 1465
get into your machine if it is not covered when it is idle. 1525

Clean the type once a week at least—every day if volume 1582
typing is done—with a clean, stiff brush. This will help produc- 1649
tion of clear-cut print-work. Also clean the platen with alcohol, 1716
closely adhering to the instructions given by an expert. Protec- 1782

(CONTINUED ON NEXT PAGE)

Preparing to Type —CONTINUED

If your machine is not equipped with a "0" on the paper guide scale:

1. Move the paper guide to the extreme left.
2. Raise paper bail away from the cylinder.
3. Hold the sheets of paper loosely with the left hand and place the paper on the paper table so that the left edge of the paper is approximately in line with the "0" mark on the cylinder scale. If your machine does not have a cylinder scale, use the paper bail scale as a guide.
4. Twirl the right cylinder knob with the thumb and first two fingers of the right hand.
5. If, after inserting the paper, you find that the left edge of the paper is not at "0" on the cylinder scale or the paper bail scale, use the paper release and move the edge of the paper to "0".
6. Move paper guide until it rests against the left edge of the paper. Note the position of the paper guide so that in the future you can set the guide to this point before inserting your paper.
7. Place the paper bail over the paper to hold it firmly against the cylinder.

STRAIGHTENING THE PAPER

Now, check your paper to see if it is straight. To do this, roll the paper forward several inches and see if the left edges of the paper line up with each other. If they do, your paper is straight—if they do not:

1. Lift the paper bail.
2. Use the paper release lever to loosen the paper.
3. Line up the left edges of the paper.
4. Reset the paper release lever and return the paper bail to typing position.

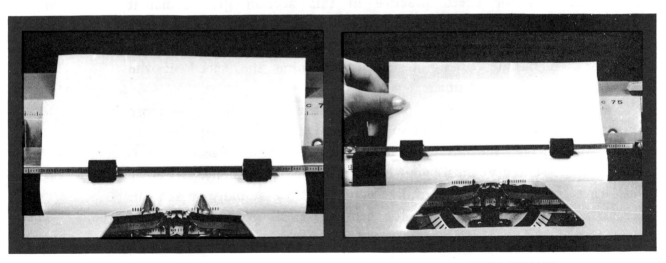

PAPER NOT STRAIGHT   STRAIGHTENING THE PAPER

The typist who can write forty or more net words a minute
should not expect to see his speed increase with every test he
takes. If, however, he will continue to write accurately and do
a sufficient quantity of repetitive practice and also practice
from new material from time to time, he will soon notice a
distinct increase in his speed.

When trying to gain the higher speeds the typist sometimes
appears to be traveling across a plateau. He fails to notice
any gain in speed whatever, and often becomes discouraged. Then
a day comes when he takes an old test over again and finds that
he has written several words a minute faster than ever before.
From that time on he begins to travel across a new and higher
speed plateau. The distance across each new plateau to the next
higher one is measured by the quantity of practice work necessary
to organize the typist's fingers for the next higher speed
plateau.

Accurate repetition is the most potent means of increasing
speed in typewriting. This applies to both word and sentence
practice. When words are used for repetitive practice they should
be carefully chosen. Those who have practiced the word exercises
of this text have already had sufficient practice of that nature.
The selections for speed practice in this section give sufficient
material to enable the typist to develop more than the average
rate of speed. These selections are counted and may be used for
five or ten minute timing tests to determine the speed of the
typist over a period of time.

The best way for the typist to use the selections to increase
his speed is to practice them in the order in which they come in
the text. Take the first sentence of the first selection and
write that sentence until you have written it without an error
at least seven times. Naturally you will occasionally make an
error. Simply keep practicing the sentence until you have written
it correctly.

520
583
648
711
770
802
861
923
988
1052
1115
1177
1242
1308
1367
1376
1435
1497
1564
1630
1696
1762
1825
1890
1954
1984
2046
2111
2173
2236
2299
2366
2380

PICA AND ELITE

Most typewriters come equipped with either elite or pica type. Elite type, which is the smaller of the two, permits the typing of 12 strokes per inch as compared with 10 strokes per inch for pica. Since most typing is done on paper that is 8½ inches wide, it is possible to type 12 x 8½, or 102 strokes across the line with an elite machine. A machine equipped with pica type, however, allows for only 10 x 8½, or 85 strokes across the line.

Notice the difference in the size of the type on the following lines:

```
ELITE: This is a sample of elite type.  Notice the size.
PICA: This is a sample of pica type.  Notice the size.
```

To determine whether your machine is equipped with elite or pica type, insert a standard-sized sheet of typing paper into the machine so that the left edge of the paper is at zero on the cylinder scale. (See illustration on page 7.) Notice the position of the right edge of the paper on the scale. The number indicated represents the number of strokes that can be typed across your paper. Therefore, if the right edge of the paper is at 102, you are using a machine that is equipped with elite type—if your paper ends at 85, your machine is equipped with pica type.

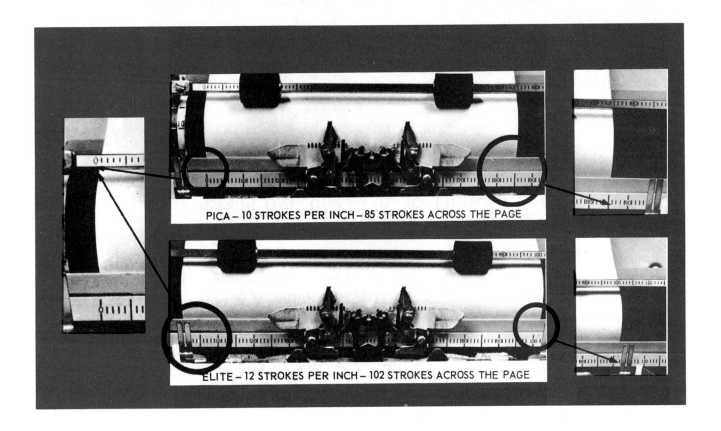

PICA — 10 STROKES PER INCH — 85 STROKES ACROSS THE PAGE

ELITE — 12 STROKES PER INCH — 102 STROKES ACROSS THE PAGE

A letter of application, like the personal history, should | *1134*
always be typed. Plain white paper is most acceptable, and it | *1197*
can be typewriter bond paper with a large envelope. If you know | *1262*
someone who is head of a department in which you would like to | *1325*
work, you may want to address your letter to him, but usually you | *1391*
would write to the person who is in charge of employment. You | *1454*
should address the person by name and title. You may be able to | *1519*
find his name in one of the directories for the field. If not, | *1583*
you can always call up the company and ask the telephone operator. | *1650*

A portfolio or presentation book is the third item you may | *1709*
want to prepare in planning your campaign. If you are applying | *1773*
for an art, photography, or writing job, you will have to present | *1839*
some concrete evidence of your ability. No matter how well you | *1903*
talk or how good your experience, an employer will want to see for | *1970*
himself what kind of work you can do. A portfolio may be simple | *2035*
or elaborate, but it should be a carefully chosen collection of | *2099*
your best samples of work. If you have had material published, | *2163*
it is wise to include that, mounting both the reproductions and | *2227*
the originals in the case of art work. | *2266*

Reprinted by permission of Glamour Magazine.

THE DEVELOPMENT OF TYPEWRITING SPEED

Accuracy is the foundation-stone upon which all high speed | *58*
in typewriting rests. It is the fundamental principle without | *121*
which the typist cannot make rapid progress, either in typewriting | *188*
speed or in the many details incidental to the duties of a typist. | *255*

Speed in typewriting may be compared to the growth of a | *311*
tree. One cannot see a tree grow from day to day, and yet, after | *377*
a sufficient length of time, the increased size of the tree may | *441*
be distinctly noted. | *462*

(CONTINUED ON NEXT PAGE)

SETTING THE MARGINS

The procedure for setting marginal stops varies considerably with the different models of typewriters. Refer to the pictures at the front of this book and the instructions on page 6 to determine the correct method for setting the marginal stops of your machine.

Before typing the exercises that follow, set your machine according to the marginal notations if they are given. Use these margins for the entire exercise unless you are otherwise instructed. If an occasional line requires more spaces than is provided for by the marginal settings, strike the margin release key (No. 18) when the carriage locks against the right margin, and type the additional letters.

LINE-SPACE REGULATOR

The line-space regulator (No. 32) adjusts the machine for single, double, or triple spacing. As you have already learned, elite type is smaller than pica, and it is therefore possible to type more strokes across the page when your machine is equipped with elite type. However, both sizes of type, whether pica or elite, will occupy the same *vertical* space–that is, six lines to the inch. In the example below, notice the difference that occurs in spacing when the copy is typed with the line-space regulator set for single, double, and triple spacing.

SINGLE SPACING

```
This is an example of
copy being typed with
single spacing.  The
line-space regulator
has been set in the "1"
position, and, as you
can see, there are no
blank lines being left
as the cylinder turns
from one line to the
next.
```

DOUBLE SPACING

```
In this example, the

copy is being typed with

the regulator in the "2"

position.  There is now

one blank line between

each line of copy.
```

TRIPLE SPACING

```
With the line-space

regulator in the "3"

position, there will

be two blank lines be-

tween each line of copy.
```

REMOVING THE PAPER

Use the paper release lever to loosen the paper. Then grasp the top of the sheet and carefully draw the paper from the machine. Return the paper release to its original position.

Another aid in your job hunt may be a private employment   1881
agency. Here you will have to pay a percentage of your first   1943
month's wages or of your annual salary, but it may save you time   2008
and effort in finding the kind of job you want in the kind of firm 2075
with which you wish to be employed. If in doubt about the reputa- 2142
bility of an employment agency, you might consult your local Better 2210
Business Bureau or Chamber of Commerce.   2250

Reprinted by permission of Glamour Magazine.

WRITING A LETTER OF APPLICATION

A letter of application is one means of obtaining an   52
appointment for an interview. It is not always necessary because   118
appointments can be made for you by school placement bureaus, by   183
friends, or by employment agencies. You, yourself, can make   244
appointments by phone, and you can even walk into personnel offices 312
without an introduction to apply for a job. Sometimes you will   376
be interviewed immediately. If you are applying for a job in a   440
distant locality, however, you will certainly need to write a   502
letter of application.   525

This letter should be short, simple and straightforward.   592
When you are writing for an out-of-town job, you should enclose   656
your personal history with the letter just as a cover letter. If   722
you are in the same city, the letter would be one way of intro-   786
ducing yourself, explaining that you are interested in a job with   852
that company, giving a clue to your qualifications, and asking for 919
an interview. You might mention that you will call his secretary   985
for an appointment, specifying a date two or three days after the 1051
arrival of your letter.   1075

(CONTINUED ON NEXT PAGE)

READY TO TYPE

| Fourth Finger | Third Finger | Second Finger | First Finger | | First Finger | Second Finger | Third Finger | Fourth Finger |

Third Row

Second Row

First Row

A S D F J K L ;

SHIFT   SHIFT

SPACE

Third Row

Second Row

First Row

Place this book on the right side of your desk.

The illustrations above and at the right show the position of the fingers on the home (or guide) keys. These keys are the keys from which all movements originate and to which the fingers always return.

Rest your fingers lightly on the home keys. Now, check yourself for the correct position at the machine:

1. Are you sitting erect in your chair with your feet resting flat on the floor?

2. Do your arms hang naturally from your shoulders, and are your elbows held comfortably close to your body?

3. Are your fingers curved, and do your hands slope parallel to the keyboard?

If you can answer "Yes" to these questions, you are ready to type!

11

JOB FINDING AIDS

You are looking for a job, you know you have something to	57
sell, now you will want to advertise yourself. Your family and	121
friends are interested in you. You will want to let them know	184
you are looking for a job. The main thing is to do this in a	246
positive way. Don't just ask if anyone knows about an opening,	310
but mention your abilities and the type of job you would like to	375
find. It is not taking advantage of friends to ask their advice	440
in a job hunt. They may know of someone or some company that	502
needs a person with just your qualifications. If they do, it's	566
to the employer's advantage to hire one personally recommended.	630
Your school or college placement office would be one of the	690
first sources of information about possible jobs. Even if you	753
have been out of school for a while, you can get help here. Watch	820
the classified advertisements in newspapers, not only for specific	887
openings, but for clues to current labor shortages and to learn	951
the prevailing wages or salaries for the work you want. Profes-	1016
sional journals and business papers also often carry classified	1080
ads of jobs available in their fields. You may even want to run	1145
an ad of your own.	1165
Once you have an idea of the kind of company you would like	1225
to work for, compile a list of individual firms by using your	1287
classified telephone directory, or specialized directories for	1350
that particular field. You would then apply directly to the	1411
companies' personnel offices for appointments for interviews.	1473
Your state employment service is an agency that offers free	1533
job placement, and in many cases, gives vocational testing and	1596
advice. In large cities the state employment service has a number	1663
of offices, sometimes different ones for different types of jobs.	1729
You will find them listed in the telephone book under the Depart-	1795
ment of Labor of your state.	1824

(CONTINUED ON NEXT PAGE)

Lesson 1

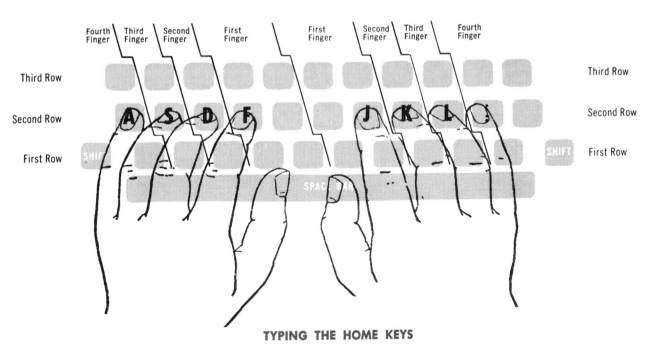

Fourth Finger · Third Finger · Second Finger · First Finger · First Finger · Second Finger · Third Finger · Fourth Finger

Third Row · Second Row · First Row

TYPING THE HOME KEYS

With a quick, sharp stroke, *tap* the letter *a* with the little finger of the left hand. Strike *s* with the next finger, *d* with the next, and *f* with the next.

With the little finger of the right hand, tap the *;* (semicolon). Strike *l* with the next finger, *k* with the next, and *j* with the next.

OPERATING THE SPACE BAR

To space between words or letters, strike the center of the space bar with a rapid inward movement of the *right* thumb.

KEEP YOUR EYES ON THE COPY IN THE BOOK and type the following line:

```
asdf ;lkj asdf ;lkj asdf ;lkj asdf ;lkj asdf ;lkj asdf ;lkj
```

HOME-KEY POSITION

Note the curve of the fingers.

12

Drill 5

GROOMING

Good grooming is as important to your job and career as the basic skills you bring with you to the office each day, and it would be well for you to read and follow the steps outlined below. 59 122 189

Start a long-range program to establish the foundation for glamour—good health. This means rest, sleep, exercise, proper diet, regular medical and dental checkups, and a reasonable pattern of living. Try to arrange regular sports sessions or dance activities such as weekends of golf, tennis, riding, swimming, perhaps using a lunch hour weekly for bowling. When possible, walk part way to and from work. 248 312 380 447 513 578 600

Budget your time, set up a tentative schedule to keep yourself and your wardrobe in good order, and keep all necessary equipment handy. It might work best to set aside one evening a week for all beauty and grooming chores, from shampoos and manicures to airing closets, mending lingerie, coffee stains, polishing shoes, and pressing dresses and skirts. Or you may prefer to scatter such tasks through the week just before bedtime or after dinner. 663 729 792 855 921 984 1049

Try to acquire a knack for providing in some degree for the inevitable emergencies. Keep an extra pair of stockings on hand; be sure you can count on at least one wrinkle-resistant dress; for an unexpected date have a flower or special necklace or scarf. 1109 1175 1238 1305

Perk yourself up and give yourself a start by something special in grooming—a good haircut and styling; a professional manicure, pedicure, or facial; a new home permanent if you can't afford a professional one; possibly even a short course by a good beauty salon or cosmetics house in everything from figure control to make-up. You may invest a small fortune in a handsome wardrobe and yet miss being beautifully dressed unless you are perfectly groomed. Basically good grooming depends upon your interest and your constant care. 1361 1425 1490 1556 1622 1689 1753 1818 1838

Reprinted by permission of Glamour Magazine.

RETURNING THE CARRIAGE

When you have finished typing a line, use the carriage return lever to bring your carriage back to the left margin.

If your machine is equipped with a high lever, reach for the carriage return lever with your palm down, your fingers braced against each other. Strike the lever with the side of your forefinger and "throw" your carriage with a swift snap of the wrist.

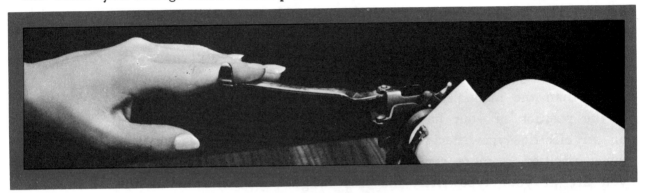

If your machine is equipped with a low lever, the same rapid action is required, but the insides of the fingers are used to operate the carriage return lever.

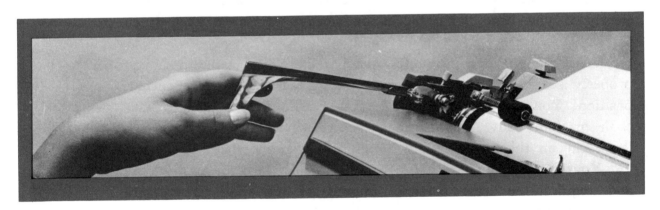

If you are using an electric typewriter the carriage return key is touched with the little finger of the right hand.

Make several correct copies of the following lines. Remember to strike each key quickly with a curved finger. Only the right thumb is used to space between words or groups of letters.

KEEP YOUR EYES ON YOUR COPY. DO NOT LOOK UP FROM YOUR BOOK.

```
as asd asdf ;l ;lk ;lkj as asd asdf ;l ;lk ;lkj as asd asdf
ask ask lads lads ask lads all all ask all lads ask all ask
```

Drill 4

YOUR TYPEWRITER AS YOUR OFFICE COMPANION

Your typewriter, as your office companion, is your best   55
friend. The better you treat it and the more you know about it,   120
the more it can do for you. So when you sit at your typewriter   184
be sure that you are comfortable, that the desk is at the proper 249
height. The height of your typewriter should be in the neighbor- 315
hood of twenty-eight to thirty inches from the floor. Of course, 381
much depends upon your own height and the kind of typewriter.   443
An electric typewriter as a rule should be two or three inches   506
lower than the manually operated typewriter. The reason for that 572
is the position of your hands upon the keyboard. Again, the keys 638
on an electric typewriter need only be touched so that a slightly 704
lower position is more comfortable for you. The more comfortable 770
you are at your typewriter, the less fatigued you will be at the 835
end of the day and the better your work will be.   884

Be sure also that your machine is immovable by fastening it   944
to the top of the table. Your typewriter will work most effi-   1007
ciently if you have bolts, blocks or wooden strips to keep it in 1073
place.   1081

With your typewriter safely anchored to the table and you   1139
properly seated in your chair, your hands will retain their correct 1207
position. You will not have to keep adjusting your machine, your 1273
chair or your body. This also makes for less fatigue on your part, 1341
less wear on the machine, and better typing production.   1397

Your notes should also be placed so that they are easily read   1459
and require the least possible amount of adjusting. There are   1522
paper holders or paper stands made for the purpose of holding   1584
notebooks or other papers in position while typing from them.   1646
Before starting to type, be sure that your notebook or whatever 1710
other material you may be using has its pages loose so that they 1775
are easily turned as you type along.   1812

Look at the above chart and locate *e* and *i*. The *e* is struck with the *d* finger; the *i* is struck with the *k* finger. In reaching for these third-row keys, unbend the finger slightly, raise it far enough to strike the desired key, and then return the finger quickly to its position on the home key. Check the illustration below for the correct technique. Note the curved finger.

REACHING FOR A
THIRD-ROW KEY

Now type the following line:

ded ded ded kik kik kik ded ded kik kik ded kik ded kik ded kik

When you can type the above line with a feeling of confidence and assurance, type the following line until you have typed it ten times correctly. Say each letter to yourself as you strike it. KEEP YOUR EYES ON THE COPY IN THIS BOOK AT ALL TIMES.

asded ;lkik asded ;lkik asded ;lkik asded ;lkik asded ;lkik

14

YOUR LETTERS ARE BEAUTIFUL

Your letters are your company's ambassadors of good will, and just as you judge a business firm by its representatives who call upon you, so other firms judge your company by the letters that you write. Many executives remark that they consider the quality of a secretary's transcript a major factor in evaluating her services. Over and over, men have said: "Please include in your booklet a few hints on making letters beautiful." 61 125 189 255 316 382 432

Here are some points to watch: See that the letter is properly centered. Make sure that the margins are as even as possible. Learn to use the tabulator for statistical and other work. If you are using a manual typewriter, develop an even touch so that there is a uniform density of printwork. 487 549 613 674 729

Your letters are a reflection of your personality, so never release a letter until you have checked it and can say to yourself: "This is a job well done. I can be proud of it." 787 851 904

Even though filing may not be one of your duties, you know its fundamentals. You're a better secretary if you can promptly produce correspondence that your boss needs. Nothing is so irritating as to have to keep a long distance caller waiting while the secretary searches for a letter, or to be told blankly that "the file can't be found." 963 1028 1088 1149 1214 1246

The executive welcomes the assurance that you and Webster agree on spelling. An incorrectly spelled or an improperly divided word is a reflection on you, your employer, and your whole organization. It is an inexcusable mistake. To guard against such errors, you keep a dictionary handy. Check any time there is a shade of doubt, and never guess at unfamiliar terms. 1304 1372 1441 1498 1562 1615

Proofread, too, for all other errors before you submit a letter for signature. 1672 1694

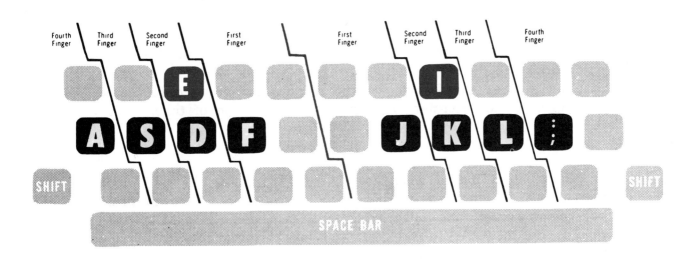

WORD LIST

Type one correct line of each of the following words. If an error is made, complete the line and then type the line again until you have succeeded in typing it without an error. ALWAYS USE THE RIGHT THUMB FOR SPACING—NEVER THE LEFT THUMB.

silks	sides	slide	skids
likes	sleds	sails	seals
desks	eased	lakes	leads
asked	dials	skill	kills

Type one correct copy of each of the following lines. If you make an error, finish the line and then type it again correctly. KEEP YOUR EYES ON YOUR COPY AS YOU TYPE.

```
led led led sled sled sled deal deal deal deals deals deals
ask ask ask asks asks asks sill sill sill sills sills sills
lad lad lad lads lads lads lake lake lake lakes lakes lakes
lid lid lid lids lids lids lead lead lead leads leads leads
kid kid kid kids kids kids seal seal seal seals seals seals
skid skids skidded skill skills skilled slake slakes slaked
dike dikes diked slide slides sailed sealed saddles saddled
```

FINGERING EXERCISE

Practice the following line until you are able to type it with facility and ease. KEEP YOUR FINGERS CURVED AND HOLD YOUR WRISTS AT THE PROPER ANGLE—SLOPING PARALLEL TO THE KEYBOARD.

```
a;sldkfjdksla;sldkfjdksla;sldkfjdksla;sldkfjdksla;sldkfjdksl
```

50 WORDS

The selections for speed practice that you find in this book will furnish sufficient material to enable you to develop more than an average speed. The selections may also be used for speed tests in order to determine your speed over a period of time.

55 WORDS

Punctuation marks were not invented to make the page look pretty, but for the reason that with them we are able to bring out our meaning, and such being the case, none should be used that is not necessary to that end. Books printed fifty years ago were sprinkled with commas.

60 WORDS

The efficient secretary is one who is not only fully capable of taking dictation and transcribing, but has acquired the skills involved in office procedures. She must be acquainted with correct grammar, must be proficient in the use of office machines, and must also present an attractive appearance.

65 WORDS

Punctuality in keeping every one of your appointments is one of the most insistent demands of business etiquette. If your working day begins officially at nine o'clock, then you have an appointment to keep every day at that hour, and not only business etiquette, but also prudence, indicate that you always be there on time.

70 WORDS

A secretary owes her employer loyalty. Since she is closely associated with him, it is logical that she should know more than the other employees about his little eccentricities, his temperament and possibly its unpleasant phases, and his private affairs. However, loyalty forbids that she should discuss any of these things with other employees.

TYPING SENTENCES

You are now ready to type your first sentence. However, before you can do so, you must learn the location of the period and the proper operation of the shift keys for capitalizing.

USING THE SHIFT KEYS

Notice that there is a shift key on each side of the keyboard. The right shift key is used to capitalize a letter that is struck with the left hand, and the left shift key is used to capitalize a letter that is struck with the right hand.

When you have gained sufficient facility in your typing, you will find that the time required to type a capital letter will gradually decrease and the operation will be performed without conscious effort on your part. As a beginner, your primary aim is to develop a smooth, even operation and to avoid any break in your typing rhythm.

To capitalize a letter that is struck with the right hand:

1. Reach for the left shift key with the *a* finger. Keep your other fingers in their correct position on the home keys.
2. *Fully* depress the left-hand shift key.
3. *While the shift key is depressed,* strike the letter to be capitalized.
4. Release the shift key and return the *a* finger to its home key.

To capitalize a letter that is struck with the left hand, follow the same procedure outlined above, using the semicolon (;) finger to depress the right shift key.

STRIKING THE PERIOD

The period is struck with the *l* finger. Curving this finger a little more than usual, move downward and a little to the right and strike the period. In all your typing, be sure to strike the space bar **twice** after a period at the end of a sentence. Now, type the following line, remembering to space **twice** after the period:

```
l.  l.  l.  all.  deal.  sill.  kill.   seal.   skill.
```

Type the following line two times correctly:

```
A lad is ill.  I asked a lass.  All lads like sleds.
```

Drill 2

ONE-MINUTE DRILLS

Type each paragraph over and over until you can type it in one minute—striving for SPEED rather than accuracy. After several *complete* writings, then try to type the same paragraph ACCURATELY during the one minute.

20 WORDS

High speeds in typewriting are built on accuracy. Without accuracy, a student cannot make progress.

25 WORDS

Accuracy is important in learning to type and in doing the tasks that every typist must perform while on a job in the office.

30 WORDS

The typing student who is able to type forty or fifty net words in a minute should not expect to see her speed increase with each test that she takes.

35 WORDS

When trying to gain the higher speeds, the student sometimes appears to be traveling across a plateau. Failing to notice any gain in her speed, she often becomes discouraged.

40 WORDS

Then a day comes when she takes an old test again and finds that she has typed several words a minute faster than before. From that time on she begins to travel across a new and higher speed plateau.

45 WORDS

Accurate repetition is the very best means you can use to build up your speed in typing. This applies to both word and sentence practice. When words are selected for repetitive practice, they should be very carefully chosen.

Lesson 2

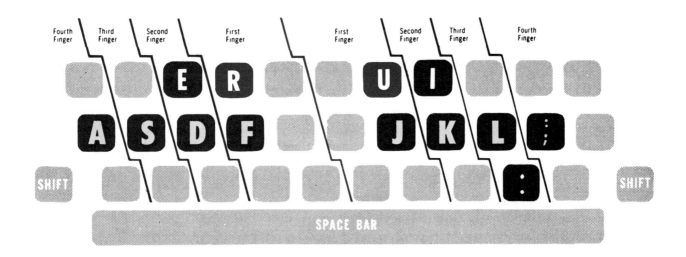

The letter *r* is struck with the *f* finger of the left hand, and *u* is struck with the *j* finger of the right hand. Locate *r* and *u* on the above chart. In reaching to the third row of keys for these letters, be sure to straighten the finger only slightly and to return the finger to its home position as soon as the letter has been typed. Type *frfrf jujuj.*

Type ten correct lines of the following line:

        frfrf jujuj frfrf jujuj frfrf jujuj frfrf jujuj frfrf jujuj

WORD LIST

Type one correct line of each of the following words. If an error is made, complete the line and then type the line again until you have succeeded in typing it without an error.

fire	freed	raid	lured
sulk	slurs	jade	lurid
rail	jails	rule	fried
lure	flake	sure	suffer

When typing, remember that you must:

1. Keep your fingers curved.
2. Strike the keys sharply.
3. Throw the carriage quickly.
4. Keep your eyes on the copy.

SHORT TIMING DRILLS

Type each of the following sentences until you are able to do so without an error. When you have typed it correctly in the allotted time, circle the words per minute indicated under that time.

	ALLOTTED TIME IN SECONDS		
15	**12**	**10**	**8**
She said she would buy the logs today 29	37	44	55
Will you tell me which way I should go 30	38	45	57
We plan to rent the house near the lake 31	39	47	58
If you like the job, you will do it well 32	40	48	60
She did not come to see us when we called 33	41	49	61
Ask the old man to tell you about his trip 33	42	50	63
One day I went to the park to hear the band 34	43	51	64
Each of you can do this work if you will try 35	44	53	66
Give them to the boys when they come to lunch 36	45	54	67
After you left, I found these books on the bus 37	46	55	69
Try to stay with us until the end of this month 37	47	56	70
We will be glad to have you go with us next time 38	48	57	72
He was away from the office when his brother came 39	49	59	73
It has been only two months since he took this job 40	50	60	75
Look over the new list and check the items you want 41	51	61	76
I know that they will be here in less than two hours 41	52	62	78
They told me that she would be at the shop to meet us 42	53	63	79
It may be that we shall not be able to return tomorrow 43	54	65	81
Please send me the name of the city in which they lived 44	55	66	82
I was sorry that she had to leave before the job was done ... 45	56	67	84
They should have told you about the fire before this time ... 45	57	68	85
We want to know if the boy broke his leg when he fell down .. 46	58	69	87
We all think it would help to have you talk to our teachers . 47	59	71	88
It is hard to tell whether the plan they made today was wise 48	60	72	90
We are able to offer you the very best price for your old car 49	61	73	91

Type one correct copy of each of the following lines. If you make an error, finish the line and then type it again correctly.

```
fire fire fire fired fired fired fairer fairer fairer

sulk sulk sulk sulks sulks sulks sulked sulked sulked

jail jail jail jails jails jails jailer jailer jailer

lark lark lark larks larks larks darker darker darker

fill fill fill fills fills fills filled filled filled

lures lures lures lured lured lured lurid lurid lurid

fled fled fled feels feels feels suffer suffer suffer
```

SENTENCES

Set your margins as follows: Pica, 11-75; Elite, 19-83; then type each of the following lines three times correctly. Space twice after a period at the end of a sentence.

```
A lurid fire failed.   A lurid fire failed.   A lurid fire failed.

Rare skill is liked.   Rare skill is liked.   Rare skill is liked.

A dull jailer sulks.   A dull jailer sulks.   A dull jailer sulks.
```

18

Lesson 52

HOW TO COMPUTE YOUR TYPING SPEED

To compute your typing speed, first determine the number of words that you typed during the typing test. To do this, find on the copy the last full line which you completed. The number after this line represents the number of strokes that you have typed to the end of that line. Add to this number any strokes on the next line that you have typed (count each letter *and space* as one stroke). Or, if you almost completed a line when time was called, subtract from the number at the end of that line the strokes that were not typed. This will constitute the total number of strokes typed.

There are five strokes to the average word. Thus, by dividing the total number of strokes by five, you can determine the number of actual words that you completed during the test. This number represents the gross words typed.

Check your copy to find the number of errors that you made. Multiply the number of errors by 10 and subtract the resulting figure from the gross words. This gives the net words typed. Divide the net words typed by the length of the test you have taken (if a 10-minute test, divide by 10; if a 5-minute test, divide by 5) and the result is your score on the basis of net words per minute.

For example:

If you type 1025 strokes on a 5-minute test and make 3 errors, your computation should be made as follows:

Divide:	Total number of strokes	1025
	by 5 to get gross words:	205
Subtract:	Total errors multiplied by 10 (3 × 10)	30
	to get net words:	175
Divide:	Net words by length of test (175 ÷ 5) to get net words per minute:	35

Lesson 3

You have already learned that *r* is struck with the *f* finger. This finger is also used to strike *g* and *t*. Locate *g* and *t* on the chart and fix their positions in your mind. Now type *fgf ftf*.

You have already learned that *u* is struck with the *j* finger. This finger is also used to strike *h* and *y*. Locate *h* and *y* on the chart and fix their positions in your mind. Now type *jhj jyj*.

Remember: The fingers striking these upper keys must be kept curved and must be returned to their home position as quickly as possible.

Type ten correct lines of the following line:

```
frf fgf ftf juj jhj jyj frf fgf ftf juj jhj jyj frf fgf ftf
```

WORD LIST

Type one correct line of each of the following words. If you make a mistake, finish the line and then type it again until you have typed it correctly.

gulfs	gifts	fright	truth
flags	jury	skater	hedge
stray	hairy	yells	layer
judge	height	yelled	right

19

Lesson 51

```
              ACHIEVEMENT TESTS ◄-------------------MAIN HEADING
                                                                      } 2 BLANK LINES (Triple Space)
          Friday, September 10, 19-- ◄------------SECONDARY HEADING
                                                                      } 2 BLANK LINES (Triple Space)
           Subject          Time       Room ◄-----COLUMN HEADINGS
                                                                      } 1 BLANK LINE (Double Space)
          Accounting         9:45       403 ◄------FIRST LINE OF COLUMN
          Bookkeeping       11:30       315
          Business English   1:30       209
          Filing I           2:00       217
          Filing II         10:30       412
          General Business   1:00       303
          Merchandising      9:00       317
          Stenography I     10:00       605
          Stenography II     2:00       306
          Typewriting        2:30       324
```

CENTERING COLUMN HEADINGS

1. Move the carriage to the beginning of the column.
2. Tap the space bar once for each two letters in the longest word in the column. Do not space for an odd letter. This will move your carriage to the midpoint of the column.
3. Backspace once for each two letters in the heading that is to appear above the column.

Tabulate the following data, centering the main and secondary headings above the tabulation and the column heading above its column:

Main Heading: SCHEDULE OF FUNCTIONS
Secondary Heading: Tuesday, January 19

Column Headings: Function   Room   Held by

Breakfast in the Crystal Gallery to be held by Sigma Pi Delta.

Luncheon in the Small Ballroom to be held by the Wingate Club.

Tea in the Coral Salon to be held by the Poetry League.

Dinner in the Silver Star Suite to be held by the Cartier Society.

Dinner in the Grand Ballroom to be held by the Artists Guild.

Type one correct line of each of the following lines. If you make an error, finish the line and then type it again correctly.

```
yell yell yell yells yells yells yelled yelled yelled

kite kite kite kites kites kites sights sights sights

tale tale tale tales tales tales trails trails trails

jugs jugs jugs judge judge judge judged judged judged

silly silly silly hilly hilly hilly jelly jelly jelly

fight fight fight fights fights fights fright frights

light light light lights lights lights lighted lighted
```

SENTENCES

Set your margins as follows: Pica, 11-75; Elite, 19-83; then type each of the following lines three times correctly. Strike the space bar twice after a period at the end of a sentence.

```
Her father hurt his left leg.  He hurt the right leg last year.

They all heard the girl say it.  The red rake is rather rusty.

He asked us if the jury had judged her guilty at the trial.
```

20

Lesson 50

HEADINGS

The headings that are typed above a tabulation may be divided into three general groups:

1. Main heading—the title of the table.
2. Secondary heading—the subheading.
3. Column heading—the title of each column.

When studying the information that follows, refer to the illustration on the **next page**.

MAIN HEADING

1. Type the main heading all in capital letters.
2. Center it above the table.
3. Allow two blank lines below the main heading.
4. A main heading that extends beyond the width of the table should be divided into two lines. In such cases, make the first line a little longer than the second.

SECONDARY HEADING

1. Capitalize the first letter of each word unless it is a preposition, article, or conjunction. If such a word begins the heading, however, it should be capitalized.
2. Center the secondary heading above the table.
3. Allow two blank lines below it.

COLUMN HEADINGS

1. Capitalize the first letter of each word unless it is a preposition, article, or conjunction. If such a word begins the heading, however, it should be capitalized.
2. Center the column heading above its column (see explanation on the next page). When the heading of a column is longer than the longest item in the body of the column, use the heading to determine the tabular setting for the column. (After the heading has been typed, however, the tabulator stop that was set for it should be cleared and a new one set to center the body of the column under the heading.)
3. If a column heading contains several words, it should be divided into two or more lines, each centered above the column.
4. Underscore the last line of the column heading.

Hospital	Founded	Number of Patients	Number of Doctors in Attendance

5. Allow one blank line before typing the table.

Lesson 4

This lesson will complete the learning of the second and third rows of keys. **Four new letters will now be added to your typing vocabulary:** *q, w, p, o.* The *q* is struck with the *a* finger, **and the *w*** is struck with the *s* finger. Practice striking *aqa sws.* As you reach for these keys, concentrate on keeping your elbows close to your body.

The semicolon (*;*) finger is used to strike *p,* and the *l* finger is used to strike *o.* Practice striking *;p; lol,* remembering to keep your elbows close to your body as you reach to the third row of keys.

Now, type ten correct lines of the following line. If you make a mistake, complete the line and then type it again.

```
aqa sws ded ;p; lol kik aqa sws ded ;p; lol kik aqa sws ded
```

WORD LIST

Type one correct line of each of the following words. Type only at the rate of speed at which you can be accurate. Do not hurry your typing.

wild	would	squall	squeals
folk	spook	equips	waffles
fowls	power	wholly	pillows
quirk	quiet	forked	ordeals
joked	polka	ghosts	quarrel

21

5. We must now determine the position for the second column:

Strike the space bar once for each letter in the longest word of the first column and once for each space between the columns. Thus, we will space 12 times for the 12 letters in the word *accommodated,* and another 12 times for the spaces to be left between the first and second column. This will give us the starting point for the second column.

6. Set the tabulator stop for the second column. Your machine is now properly set for typing the above table.

Using the method just outlined, tabulate the following exercises. Single space Exercise 1, double space Exercise 2.

EXERCISE 1		EXERCISE 2	
WORDS THAT HAVE GROWN TOGETHER		**CHRISTMAS PARTY COMMITTEE**	
antechamber	blindfold	Harold Fisher	Sales
armchair	bookcase	William T. Brooks	Purchasing
backdoor	bookkeeper	Mary Henderson	Payroll
bathtub	businesslike	L. Charles Tremont	Bookkeeping
bedroom	lawmaker	Elizabeth Collin	Secretary
bedside	meanwhile	Mary Chambers	Secretary
bedtime	newsdealer	Alice G. Vickers	Typist
beefsteak	playwright	Gertrude Blanchard	Receptionist
blackmail	postmark	Louis Bellford	Messenger
bygone	scrapbook	B. P. Leiland	Mail Room
classmate	turnover		
commonplace	viewpoint		
copyright	worksheet		
farsighted	workout		
handbook	yearbook		

Type one correct copy of each of the following lines. If you make an error, finish the line and then type it again correctly.

```
pal pal pal pals pals pals pail pail pail pails pails pails
oak oak oak oaks oaks oaks oral oral oral quits quits quits
old old old gold gold gold told told told holds holds holds
pad pad pad pads pads pads pray pray pray world world world
spoil spoil spoil quill quill quill foil foil foil foils
swell swell swell drops drops drops warp warp warp warps
quirk quirk quirk fold fold fold wisp wisp wisp quails
```

SENTENCES

Type each of the following lines two times correctly.

```
We were sure we saw four quail fly through the quiet forest.
She quietly read the paper while she waited for her sister.
We all feel that these eight pupils are equal to the tasks.
```

SUPPLEMENTARY SENTENCES

Set your margins as follows: Pica, 16-70; Elite, 24-78.

```
The forests were dark.  The forests were dark.
They like to play quoits.  They like to play quoits.
His paper showed that he was qualified for the work.
```

22

Lesson 48

ARRANGING TWO-COLUMN TABLES

As already stated, the aim in tabulation is to arrange columns so that they are neatly and attractively spaced. To do this, you can employ the most commonly-used method for planning the positioning of columns in table form—the Backspace Method

BACKSPACE METHOD

The Backspace Method is simply an extension of the centering technique you have been using, in which a word is centered by backspacing once for every two letters in the word.

Let us assume that we wish to set up our tabulated material as in this example:

WORDS OFTEN MISSPELLED

accommodated	interfere
affect	knowledge
bureaus	maneuver
disappoint	noticeable
develop	occurred
embarrass	parallel
familiar	referred
hygiene	separated

1. Determine the longest word in each column.

    accommodated   noticeable

2. Starting at the center of the page, backspace once for each two letters in these words. Do not backspace for an odd letter, and do not allow for any spaces between words.

    ac co mm od at ed no ti ce ab le

3. We must now provide for the spaces between the two columns—the intercolumn. (In this example, we will arbitrarily allow 12 spaces.) To do this, backspace once for each two spaces to be left between columns. (Backspace 6 times for the 12 spaces in this example.) The carriage is now positioned at the starting point for the first column.

4. Set the left margin at the point located in Step 3.

Lesson 5

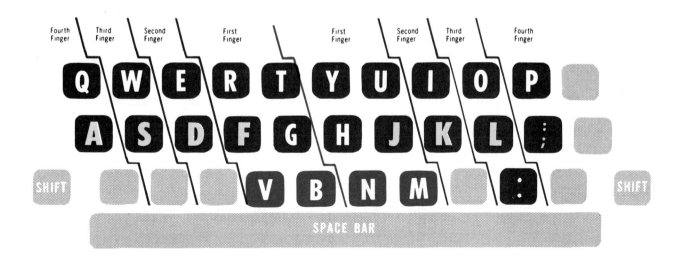

Both *b* and *v* are struck with the *f* finger. The reach from *f* to *b* is a long one, and requires a great deal of practice before you are able to strike it with facility. Locate the *b* and *v* keys on the above chart. Now, strike *fbfvf*. Practice this several times. Now, locate *m* and *n* on the chart. Notice that both *m* and *n* are struck with the *j* finger. Typing slowly, strike *jnjmj*.

Type ten correct lines of the following line:

```
fbfvf jnjmj fbfvf jnjmj fbfvf jnjmj fbfvf jnjmj fbfvf jnjmj
```

WORD LIST

Type one correct line of each of the following words. If you make a mistake, finish the line and then, typing more carefully, type the line correctly. Strive for accurate, even stroking.

```
build      bluffs      smokes      animals
women      proved      banner      velvets
veils      squint      normal      janitor
small      movers      sublet      bravery
```

Before typing the following exercise, take a moment to check your position at the typewriter.

1. Are you sitting erect in your chair with your feet resting flat on the floor?

2. Do your arms hang naturally from your shoulders, and are your elbows held comfortably close to your body?

3. Are your fingers curved, and do your hands slope parallel to the keyboard?

Lesson 47

ARRANGING ONE-COLUMN TABLES

A one-column table should be typed so that the longest item is centered on the line. Follow this procedure:

1. Select the longest item in the column to be typed.
2. Move the carriage to the center of the line and, using the centering method described on page 30, backspace once for every two letters in this longest item.
3. Set left margin stop at this point.
4. Type the column, starting each item at the left margin.

EXERCISE 1

Center the following list, single spaced, on a full sheet of paper.

Purchase Orders
Invoices
Statements
Interoffice Memos
Telegrams
Postal Cards

EXERCISE 2

Center the following list, double spaced, on a full sheet of paper.

Student's Handbook
World Atlas
Standard Dictionary
Dictation Manual
Secretarial Guide

EXERCISE 3

Center the following list, single spaced, on the top half of a sheet of paper. In planning your vertical placement, base your figures on the fact that there are only 33 lines on a half-sheet.

Mr. John Bailey, Mrs. Ruth Gordon, Miss Catherine Ames, Mr. Charles McNichols, Mr. S. Brookhaven, Mr. Thomas Jackson, Mr. Paul Harrison

EXERCISE 4

Center the following list, single spaced, on the bottom half of the sheet of paper:

New York, Washington, Ohio, New Mexico, California, Oregon, Nebraska, Minnesota, Louisiana, Illinois, Kansas, Kentucky, Utah, Texas

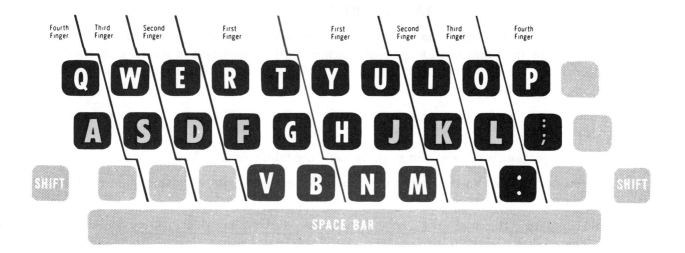

Type one correct copy of each of the following lines.

DO NOT LOOK UP FROM YOUR COPY AS YOU THROW YOUR CARRIAGE.

```
buff buff buff buffs buffs buffs muff muff muff muffs muffs
sink sink sink sinks sinks sinks link link link links links
bark bark bark barks barks barks lava lava lava veals veals
tune tune tunes tonal tonal tonal trunk trunk trunks trunks
helm helm helm warms warms warms pave pave pave paved paved
many many many money money money mean mean mean named named
junk junk junk junks junks junks bang bang bang bangs bangs
```

SENTENCES

Type each of the following lines two times correctly:

```
Many brave men will die when the battle is fought here tonight.
The farmer built a new red barn on the land he had just bought.
Have them thank the young boys for giving the money to the man.
```

SUPPLEMENTARY SENTENCES

Set your margins as follows: Pica, 17-69; Elite, 25-77.

```
He sailed in an old junk.  He sailed in an old junk.
They walked over the links.  They walked over the links.
The farmer built a big barn.  The farmer built a big barn.
```

Lesson 46

TABULATING COLUMNS

Until now, you have used the tabulating mechanism on your machine for business-letter indentation only. You must now learn to set your machine for the tabulation of several columns. To gain facility in the use of the tabulator key, type the drills below until you are able to use the tabulator key without hesitation.

Before typing each exercise, prepare your machine according to the instructions included with the exercise. To do this:

1. Clear all previously set tabulator stops by using the tabulator clear key.

2. Move your carriage to the position indicated for each column and depress the tabulator set key.

3. In typing the columns of the exercise, depress the tabulator key after each word and do not release the key until your carriage comes to a complete stop.

4. KEEP YOUR EYES ON YOUR COPY AT ALL TIMES.

EXERCISE 1

For Pica: Left margin at 15. Tab set at 32, 50, and 68
   Elite: Left margin at 18. Tab set at 39, 60, and 81

same	long	they	more
asks	name	dale	here
sent	open	down	your
when	just	from	know
come	make	very	must

VERTICAL PLACEMENT

In setting up material *on a blank page,* your objective is to center the material in such a way that the margins at the top and bottom of the page will be the same. Following the procedure outlined below will enable you to accomplish this.

1. Count the number of lines that the material will occupy. Take into consideration all extra lines required for double spacing.

2. Since there are 6 typewritten lines per inch (with both pica and elite type), an 8½ x 11-inch page will contain 66 lines from top to bottom. Therefore subtract from 66 the number of lines needed for the tabulation to determine the total number of lines available for the top and bottom margins.

3. Divide this total number of lines by 2 to determine the number of lines to allow for the top margin.

Lesson 6

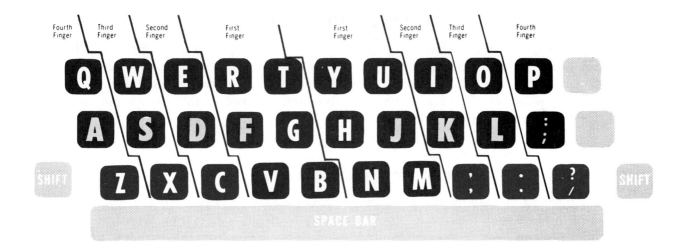

This lesson completes the learning of the basic keyboard.

On the above chart, locate *z, x,* and *c.* Notice that the *z* is struck with the *a* finger, *x* is struck with the *s* finger, and *c* is struck with the *d* finger. Practice striking *aza sxs dcd.*

Now locate the positions of the diagonal (/) and the comma (,). The diagonal is struck with the semicolon (;) finger and the comma is struck with the *k* finger. The period, as you already know, is struck with the *l* finger. Practice striking *;/; l.l k,k.*

Type ten correct lines of the following line:

```
aza sxs dcd ;/; l.l k,k aza sxs dcd ;/; l.l k,k aza sxs dcd
```

WORD LIST

Typing slowly and accurately, type one correct line of each of the following words.

zone	foxes	black	clock
exit	amaze	evict	glaze
quiz	curls	scowl	expel
cozy	mixed	extra	brick

Type two correct lines of the following line. Always space ONCE after a comma.

```
Buy some books, pencils, pens, crayons, and clips for the boys.
```

25

Lesson 45

INTRODUCTION TO TABULATION

Tabulation is simply the process of typing columns. As a typist or secretary, you will frequently be called upon to type columns either in the body of a letter or in a business form. A knowledge of tabulation techniques will enable you to set up these columns so that they are neatly and attractively placed on the page. Learn the procedures outlined in this section and you will always be proud of your finished work.

USE OF THE TABULATING MECHANISM

The tabulating mechanism is one of the greatest time-saving devices on the typewriter. It enables you to move your carriage to a pre-set position with just one motion. You first use this mechanism in Lesson 7 where you are required to indent five spaces from the margin at the beginning of each sentence. By using the tabulator key, you eliminate the necessity of striking the space bar five times for each indentation.

Familiarize yourself with the location and operation of these three parts on your typewriter:

1. Tabulator Clear Key (No. 25 or 38)
2. Tabulator Set Key (No. 17)
3. Tabulator Bar or Key (No. 19)

Locate each of these parts on your typewriter by referring to the photographs at the front of this book (page 4).

INDENTING FOR PARAGRAPHS

1. Clear all previously set tabulator stops. To do this, move your carriage to the right margin and depress the tabulator clear key. *While this key is depressed,* move your carriage back to the left margin. Then release the clear key. (If your typewriter is equipped with a *total* tabulator clear key (No. 38) it is not necessary to move the carriage.

2. Using the space bar, move the carriage five spaces from the left margin. Depress the tabulator set key. You have now set your machine for a paragraph indentation of five spaces.

3. Move the carriage back to the left margin and depress the tabulator key. (Use the little finger to depress the tabulator key. However, if your typewriter has a tabulator *bar,* use the *j* finger.) Do not release the key until your machine has come to a complete rest. Your carriage has now moved into position so that you may type the first word of the indented sentence.

Now that you have set this tabulator stop for the first indentation, you need only to depress the tabulator key whenever you wish to indent. This setting will hold until it is released by the tabulator clear key.

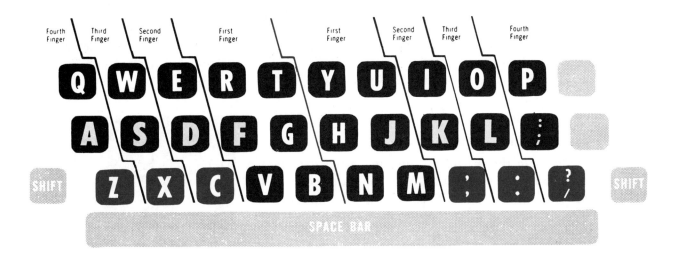

Type one correct copy of each of the following lines. If you make an error, finish the line and then type it again correctly.

```
box box box jazz jazz jazz calix calix calix affix affix
mix mix mix cook cook cook cooks cooks cooks blaze blaze
zoo zoo zoo quiz quiz quiz maxim maxim maxim corks corks
cap cap cap next next next gazes gazes gazes razed razed
dot dot dot cask cask cask amaze amaze amaze child child
cry cry cry back back back oxide oxide oxide taxes taxes
wax wax wax exit exit exit voice voice voice click click
```

SENTENCES

Type two correct lines of each of the following lines:

```
The busy old men did not stop work when the clock struck six.
Not one of the four clerks could move the heavy black box.
The boy who has the best mark in the class will get a prize.
```

SUPPLEMENTARY SENTENCES

Set your margins as follows: Pica, 15-72; Elite, 23-79.

```
The clock struck six.  The clock struck six.
A dozen men called up.  A dozen men called up.
Four clerks were excused.  Four clerks were excused.
```

26

Lesson 44

CHANGING THE RIBBON

Before assuming that a ribbon is completely worn out, move the indicator lever to the opposite color and test the ribbon. Very often a one-color ribbon may be completely worn out in the "blue" position and never used in the "red" position.

If the ribbon appears to need replacement, proceed as follows:

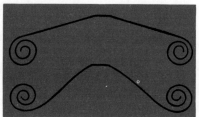

1. Carefully study, in detail, how the present ribbon is threaded into the machine. Note, in particular, whether the ribbon spools are wound from the outer edges of the typewriter, as in the top illustration at the right, or from the inner edges, as in the bottom illustration.

2. Raise the ribbon carrier by placing the ribbon indicator to the "red" position and press any two keys until the type bars lock together. This will keep the ribbon carrier in the raised position.

3. Wind the old ribbon onto one spool. If the spool cannot be rotated, use the ribbon release lever with which some machines are equipped.

4. Remove the ribbon from the ribbon carrier and lift the spools from the ribbon cups. Detach the old ribbon from the empty spool.

5. Unwind about 12 inches of new ribbon and place the new spool in the ribbon cup that permits it to unwind as explained in Step 1 above. If you are inserting a two-color ribbon, the red half must be on the bottom.

6. Attach the end of the new ribbon to the empty spool, making sure that the ribbon is not twisted.

7. Thread the ribbon through the ribbon carrier.

8. Unlock the two keys that were used to raise the carrier. Return the ribbon indicator lever to the "blue" position if you wish.

Lesson 7

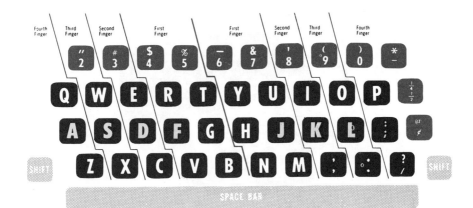

In the following fingering exercise, *s2s* indicates that the figure *2* is struck with the same finger that is used to strike *s*. In the same way, *d3d* means that *d* and *3* are struck with the same finger, etc. Notice that the small letter *l* is used for the figure 1. (Rules for the use of numbers and characters are given on pages 64 through 68, and 70 and 71.)

Type ten correct lines of the following line:

```
s2s d3d f4f f5f ;-; ;0; 191 k8k j7j j6j ;/; ;¢; ;½;
```

> ## SPACING AFTER PUNCTUATION MARKS
>
> Strike the space bar TWICE after a colon and any mark of punctuation at the end of a sentence (a period, a question mark, or an exclamation point).
>
> Strike the space bar ONCE after a period at the end of an abbreviation, and after a comma or a semicolon.
>
> Do not space before or after a hyphen used in a hyphenated word. However, when the hyphen is used as a dash, use either a single hyphen with a space before and after it, or two hyphens with no space before, between, or after the hyphens.

Before typing the sentences that follow, read the instructions on page 76 subtitled "Use of the Tabulating Mechanism" and "Indenting for Paragraphs." Set your margins as follows: Pica, 12-74; Elite, 20-82; then type each sentence five times correctly.

Sentence One

```
On April 19 we received your invoice C3950 for 1487 bags,
305 sacks, and 159 cartons.  These were shipped April 20.
```

TAKING CARE OF YOUR TYPEWRITER

Just a few moments of your care each day will bring you years of extra use from your typewriter. To obtain the maximum use and satisfaction from your machine, follow these suggestions:

AS YOU TYPE

1. Never type on a single sheet of paper. Reduce wear on cylinder by always using a second sheet—called a "backing sheet"—in back of your paper.
2. When erasing, move carriage to extreme right or left to prevent erasure particles from falling in the machine. (See photograph on page 61.)
3. Release paper release lever when typewriter is not in use.

EVERY DAY

1. Dust exterior parts with a brush or lint-free cloth.
2. Dust under machine so that particles will not be blown into machine from below.
3. Wipe carriage rails with a dry cloth.
4. Clean type with dry, stiff brush.
5. Cover machine at the end of the day to keep out dust.

ONCE A WEEK

1. Wipe carriage rails with a cloth that is slightly moistened with oil.
2. Clean type with any standard type-cleaning fluid.
3. Clean cylinder and paper bail rolls with denatured alcohol or carbon tetrachloride.

Sentence Two

We have this date shipped your order of May 3 for 28½ dozen pencils at 25 cents per dozen, and 39 dozen pads at 29 cents each.

Sentence Three

Our records show that we sold 185 suits and 391 dresses by January 15 as against 109 suits and 306 dresses for the same period last year. Our sales force was decreased by 28 men and 30 women.

Sentence Four

Twenty-four copies of your latest 12-page catalog are to be sent to Mrs. Jane Roth, 9206 Fourth Avenue, Boston 29, Massachusetts, and Mr. R. Dunn, 5958 East 47 Street, Los Angeles 30, California.

Sentence Five

The dealer sold 5/7 of a bushel for 56¢, 32 3/5 cases for 13¢ per case, and the balance of the order at a flat rate of 47¢ per pound, even though it cost him 8¢ per pound for shipment.

Sentence Six

Your 38-page pamphlet reached me on June 9, and I am happy to enclose my order for 47 leather wallets and 60 silver key chains. I would also appreciate it if you would quote prices on 72 storage units that measure 36 by 59½ inches.

Lesson 43

TYPING STENCILS

PREPARE THE COPY

PREPARE THE TYPEWRITER

PREPARE THE STENCIL

TYPE THE STENCIL

CORRECTING ERRORS
ON STENCILS

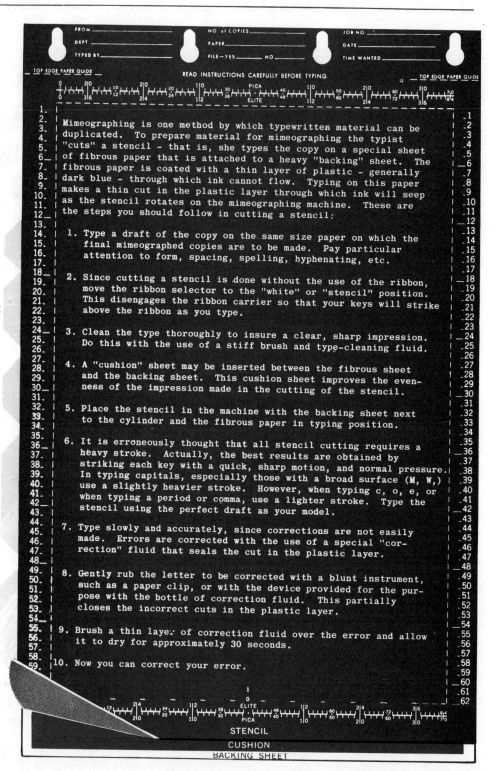

FROM _____ NO of COPIES _____ JOB NO. _____

DEPT _____ PAPER _____ DATE _____

TYPED BY _____ FILE—YES _____ NO _____ TIME WANTED _____

TOP EDGE PAPER GUIDE   READ INSTRUCTIONS CAREFULLY BEFORE TYPING   TOP EDGE PAPER GUIDE

Mimeographing is one method by which typewritten material can be duplicated. To prepare material for mimeographing the typist "cuts" a stencil - that is, she types the copy on a special sheet of fibrous paper that is attached to a heavy "backing" sheet. The fibrous paper is coated with a thin layer of plastic - generally dark blue - through which ink cannot flow. Typing on this paper makes a thin cut in the plastic layer through which ink will seep as the stencil rotates on the mimeographing machine. These are the steps you should follow in cutting a stencil:

1. Type a draft of the copy on the same size paper on which the final mimeographed copies are to be made. Pay particular attention to form, spacing, spelling, hyphenating, etc.

2. Since cutting a stencil is done without the use of the ribbon, move the ribbon selector to the "white" or "stencil" position. This disengages the ribbon carrier so that your keys will strike above the ribbon as you type.

3. Clean the type thoroughly to insure a clear, sharp impression. Do this with the use of a stiff brush and type-cleaning fluid.

4. A "cushion" sheet may be inserted between the fibrous sheet and the backing sheet. This cushion sheet improves the evenness of the impression made in the cutting of the stencil.

5. Place the stencil in the machine with the backing sheet next to the cylinder and the fibrous paper in typing position.

6. It is erroneously thought that all stencil cutting requires a heavy stroke. Actually, the best results are obtained by striking each key with a quick, sharp motion, and normal pressure. In typing capitals, especially those with a broad surface (M, W,) use a slightly heavier stroke. However, when typing c, o, e, or when typing a period or comma, use a lighter stroke. Type the stencil using the perfect draft as your model.

7. Type slowly and accurately, since corrections are not easily made. Errors are corrected with the use of a special "correction" fluid that seals the cut in the plastic layer.

8. Gently rub the letter to be corrected with a blunt instrument, such as a paper clip, or with the device provided for the purpose with the bottle of correction fluid. This partially closes the incorrect cuts in the plastic layer.

9. Brush a thin layer of correction fluid over the error and allow it to dry for approximately 30 seconds.

10. Now you can correct your error.

STENCIL

CUSHION

BACKING SHEET

73

Lesson 8

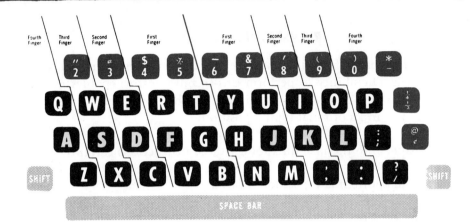

The finger reaches in this exercise are the same as those used in Lesson Seven, except that the shift key is depressed before striking each character key. To write s"s simply strike s, then depress the right-hand shift key and strike the sign for the quotation marks, after which release the shift key and again strike s. Proceed in the same way with the remainder of the exercise, depressing the right shift key when the special character is struck with a finger of the left hand, and the left shift key when the character is struck with a finger of the right hand. (Rules for the use of these characters are given on pages 70 and 71.)

Type ten correct lines of the following line:

s"s d#d f$f f%f ;*; ;); l(l k'k j&j j_j ;?; ;@; ;¼; ;:;

Set your margins as follows: Pica, 9-77; Elite, 17-85; then type each of the following sentences five times correctly.

Note in particular the spacing used before and after each character.

Sentence One

The girl's employer said, "Send Model #130 to Smith & Sons and include a bill for $146.15."

Sentence Two

The merchant marked piece #73 to sell at $3.75 a yard and then advertised it extensively in the local paper.

Sentence Three

The bank offered 2¼% interest on balances of over $10,000.

Sentence Four

The sign (*) was frequently used by the author to indicate the sources from which he drew his facts.

29

REINSERTING PAPER

It is possible to remove paper from the machine and then reinsert it in such a way that its removal cannot be detected. The ability to perform this technique thus enables the typist to either continue with a letter that was removed before it was finished or correct an error that was not noticed while the paper was in its original typing position.

To reinsert your paper into the machine, follow these instructions carefully:

1. Insert paper to the approximate position desired.

2. Make certain the card holders are lowered.

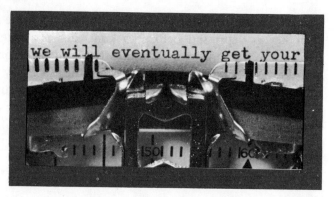

3. Using the paper release, straighten the paper, meanwhile shifting it until an "*i*" or "*l*" in your copy is in perfect alignment with the calibration marks on the alignment scale.

4. Using the variable line spacer, move the cylinder until the original line of typing is even with the top of the alignment bar.

5. Check the accuracy of your reinsertion by putting the ribbon selector in stencil position and type over one of the original letters. The faint impression that results will indicate whether further adjustments are necessary.

6. When the strikeover indicates perfect alignment, return the ribbon selector to normal position and continue typing.

If you are reinserting the paper to make a correction, do not try to correct both the original and carbon copies at the same time. Instead, insert each sheet separately and make the correction.

TYPING ON RULED LINES

To type on a ruled line, use the variable line spacer when rolling the paper to the correct typing position. This correct position will be found by rolling the cylinder until the ruled line is slightly below the alignment bar. In this position, the letters to be typed will not cross the ruled line or be too far above it.

Example: Proper typing on a ruled line.

Sentence Five

The girl's record was a good one and she received a position with the house of J. K. Newton & Co.

Sentence Six

To <u>underscore</u> a word, type the word, <u>backspace</u> for each letter in the word, and then insert the underscore.

Sentence Seven

If you buy 10 yards at one time, the price is $2.50 a yard. If, however, you buy only ½ of a yard, the goods are sold @ 93¢ a foot.

KEYBOARD MASTERY SECTION

If you have thoroughly practiced all the lessons to this point, you can now type by touch with a fair degree of facility. Without looking at the keyboard, you can type any word with a little conscious effort. However, for really rapid typing, it is necessary to automatize this skill to the point where there is *no* conscious effort—where you see the words, and your fingers respond automatically and accurately.

The lessons that follow are planned to accomplish just this—to develop your speed and accuracy. Notice that each drill is designed to develop a particular skill. Practice these drills diligently and you will develop correct habits from the start. Remember, repetition builds speed, accuracy, and efficiency.

CENTERING

On page 9 you learned that 102 letters can be typed across the line of an 8½-inch page on an elite machine, 85 letters on a pica machine. Dividing these numbers by 2 gives 51 as the center point of the elite machine and 42 as the center point of the pica machine. Remember these numbers—51 and 42—so that whenever you have to center any material on 8½-inch paper, you can immediately move your carriage to the center position.

Having set the carriage to the center position, backspace once for every two letters *or spaces* in the words to be centered. Thus, to center the words *ALPHABET REVIEW* on the following page, mentally spell out the heading as you backspace once for each two letters or spaces. If there is a single letter left over, do not backspace for it.

In this example you would backspace seven times: *Al ph ab et space-r ev ie*. Then, from this point, type the heading and it will be centered on your page.

30

PROPER SPACING FOR MARKS OF PUNCTUATION AND CHARACTERS (Continued)

	No space before or after an apostrophe.	I can't find Mary's record. I'll check it at two o'clock.
( )	Space once before typing the opening parenthesis and once after typing the closing parenthesis, but do not space between the parentheses and the words they enclose.	In the illustration given (see below) the purpose is made clear.
	Type the comma, semicolon, colon, and dash after the closing parenthesis.	Although we are not satisfied with our order (there are too many broken pieces), we are paying the bill.
	A period, question mark, or exclamation point is typed outside the parentheses when it punctuates the entire sentence. These marks of punctuation are placed inside the parentheses when they punctuate the enclosed material.	They met at the Waldorf (Hotel). We have waited 30 days (doesn't it seem longer?) for the package.
&	One space before and after the ampersand.	Mark & Sons
#	Do not space between the number sign and the number it identifies.	Style #34, Bill #45
$	No space between the dollar sign and the number it identifies.	We have a bill for $35.
%	No space between the percent sign and the number it identifies.	A discount of 18%.
*	Often used to refer to a footnote. Do not space between the asterisk and the word that precedes it.	This article* appeared two months ago.
@	One space before and after the "at" sign.	4 @ $3.50
¢	Do not space between the cent sign and the number it identifies.	15 lbs @ 18¢
/	When used to express a fraction, do not space between the numbers of the fraction and the diagonal.	A total of 4 3/8 inches.

Lesson 9

ALPHABET REVIEW

EXERCISE 1

a   at an as am and are arm air ace ape art any age add ask
aim able away also axle acre after about acquit adjusts

b   be bin bed buy ban bag bite brag ball baby blaze braved

c   cat cup cry can cost come cell cord care city cede copy

d   dad did dot dry die dye draw desk daze dish dawn dreads

e   elf eat eye end ere ebb eel eggs even equal extra enjoy

EXERCISE 2

e   evil each earn east every erode edges exile elite elder

f   for fan few fit fox fuse fork find from fear fled froze

g   get got gas gag gem give gang grab gone gnaw glue grope

h   her him how hat had held help hope hate hash here hilly

i   if in it is ire ill irk ivy ice ilk imp idea into irons
inn idle iris items index inches italic invited insides

EXERCISE 3

j   jam jet jug job jut jeer joys jerk jazz just jibe judge

k   keg kind kite keys knew know knob knee king kinks knife

l   low lax law lip lied lazy live long lamp liquid lullaby

m   met mop mud milk maze many make much moody major mailed

n   no nut now new next navy none noun nine need nice noble

o   on of or oil off out our one own old odd oath obey onto

31

Lesson 41

HELPFUL HINTS TO THE TYPIST

PROPER SPACING FOR MARKS OF PUNCTUATION AND CHARACTERS

.	Space twice after a period at the end of a sentence. Space once after a period at the end of an abbreviation.	Order now. It's not too late. Mr. C. L. Bradley
?	Space twice after a question mark.	Did you go? No.
!	Space twice after an exclamation point.	No! Yes! Not really!
:	Space twice after a colon.	as follows: bills, clips, and pencils.
,	Space once after a comma.	Invoices, bills, and statements.
;	Space once after a semicolon.	All orders must be entered; all bills must be paid.
"	No space between opening quotation marks and the first word of the quoted material. Space once after the closing marks if they are not at the end of a sentence.	She marked "paid" on the bill.
	A period or a comma is typed *before* the quotation marks.	"The book," she said, "is very interesting."
	If the quoted material is a question or an exclamation, but the rest of the sentence is not, type the question mark or exclamation point *inside* the quotation marks.	I heard her ask, "Where are you going?" The man said, "What a beautiful sight!"
	If the entire sentence is a question or an exclamation, type the question mark or exclamation point *outside* the quotation marks.	Who purchased "Typing Techniques"?
	The semicolon, colon, and dash are always typed outside the quotation marks.	The following are considered "standard equipment":
--	When using two hyphens to indicate a dash, do not space before, between, or after the hyphens. When a single hyphen is used as a *dash*, space once before and after it.	He came today--didn't you meet him? He came today - didn't you see him?
-	No space before or after the hyphen.	A first-class job. Second-hand car.

(CONTINUED ON NEXT PAGE)

Lesson 10

ALPHABET REVIEW

EXERCISE 4

o | only oxen owes once over okays opens older oftener ogre

p | pen pay put pan pop pray part prim pole pace path proper

q | quit quake quota quick quiet queens quest quart quality

r | rag red ran rib rob ramp rose real rave ripe raze refer

s | see sea sit sob sew sale suit such sort sell seen store

t | two tie tap tea the tax try this talk tools truth teach.

EXERCISE 5

u | up use urn urge upon used untie upper under utter until

v | vie vim vet van visa vote very vast verb voice visitors

w | we was way why wit war with wall well white where which

x | axe lax oxen boxer taxes exit extra except buxom flaxen

y | you yam yet yes year yard yoke yours yarns yearly young

z | zoo zip zeal zing zones zonal zodiac zircon zigzag zinc

EXERCISE 6   **FIRST FINGER DRILL**

fur jug ban tag nun toy rut bin jam hum fit jut try get

jury veto bury nine hurt brunt gravy mount thumb thorny

norm jamb verb bent rush grey broth rumor number gutter

bath mart fuel bunt yelp grab rift graft mumble through

youth birth grunt hunter brogue trysts frighten nurture

froth jumbo thrust bounty trying ferries voyages yeasts

Lesson 40

CHARACTERS NOT ON THE KEYBOARD

!	**EXCLAMATION POINT**	Type the apostrophe, backspace, and type the period. On some machines, it is possible to hold down the space bar with the left thumb, depress the shift key with the left hand, and type the apostrophe and then the period without backspacing.	Indeed! Yes!
=	**EQUAL**	Strike the hyphen, backspace, depress the shift key *slightly* and type the hyphen a second time.	12 x 12 = 144
÷	**DIVIDE**	Strike the hyphen, backspace, and strike the colon.	100 ÷ 2 = 50
—	**SUBTRACT**	Type the hyphen with a space before and after it.	144 - 44 = 100
×	**MULTIPLY**	Strike the small letter "*x*" with a space before and after.	16 x 5 = 80
°	**DEGREE**	Use ratchet release, turn cylinder toward you one-half space and strike the small letter "*o*" without spacing after the number. Return ratchet release to normal typing position and turn cylinder back to original line of typing.	38° North
'	**MINUTES OR FEET**	Strike the apostrophe without spacing after the number.	6'4" long
"	**SECONDS OR INCHES**	Strike the quotation marks without spacing after the number.	
said[2]	**RAISED FIGURES**	Use ratchet release, turn cylinder toward you one-half space and insert the desired number or letter. Return ratchet release to normal typing position and turn cylinder back to original line of typing. The bottom of the raised number or letter should be on a line with the top of a lower case letter.	book[2] had merit.
H_2O	**SUBNUMERALS**	Use ratchet release, turn cylinder away from you one-half space and insert the desired number. Return ratchet release to normal typing position and turn cylinder back to original line of typing. A subnumeral may also be inserted by depressing the shift key halfway before striking the desired number.	H_2SO_4
c/o	**CARE OF**	Strike the small letter "*c*", the diagonal, and the small letter "*o*".	c/o Postmaster
--	**DASH**	Strike the hyphen twice, without spacing before or after it. The dash may also be typed by striking the hyphen once, spacing both before and after it.	Now--not later. Now - not later.
+	**PLUS SIGN**	Type the hyphen, backspace, use the ratchet release to roll the paper slightly upward, and strike the apostrophe repeatedly while returning the roller.	18 + 20 = 38
7/8	**FRACTIONS**	See page 66.	
III	**ROMAN NUMERALS**	See page 68.	

EXERCISE 7   FIRST FINGER DRILL

```
All through the night the trains hurry along the river.
The forty-nine brave men ejected the enemy by the fort.
Try to do your typing with a smooth and an even rhythm.
They bought the gun, but the barrel was ruined by rust.
The boy's mother told him to be kind in judging others.
Have them join you tonight in the room above the store.
```

EXERCISE 8   FOURTH FINGER DRILL

```
pet que zip map ply ape quit path quick zoom pray azure
aqua people plaza hazy quiet mazes queens bazaar piazza
size prizes pamper quart pupil seize plant happy appear
awake quaint primps pepper equips spring zigzag popular
zeal queer plaque opal spawns hazel quote crazy happens
quest razor acquaint pique horizon racquet quiz puppies
```

EXERCISE 9   FOURTH FINGER DRILL

```
The prize was awarded to the zealous and excited pupil.
Was the blazing fire in the paper mill quickly put out?
The citizens were happy to answer the appeals for help.
They were amazed to see the quaint, antique pepper pot.
Seize the opportunity to improve your typing technique.
Did many people appear at the masquerade with costumes?
```

PARAGRAPH STRESSING ALPHABET REVIEW

One day, about six years ago, I walked into my local store	58
to buy a saw with which to cut some new lumber. As I looked at	122
the large stock on display, I caught sight of an Ajax saw. I	184
was amazed by the low price of this saw and I spoke to a clerk	247
about it. He told me that the Ajax was the very best saw on	308
the market and, acting on his advice, I bought it. The Ajax	369
saw has served me well during these many years and I have good	432
reason to be glad that I followed the advice given by that clerk.	498

ROMAN NUMERALS

Roman numerals are easily typed by using capital letters. For numbers over 5,000, note how the *V* or *M* is overscored by using the underscore key.

1	I	11	XI	30	XXX	400	CD
2	II	12	XII	40	XL	500	D
3	III	13	XIII	50	L	600	DC
4	IV	14	XIV	60	LX	700	DCC
5	V	15	XV	70	LXX	900	CM
6	VI	16	XVI	80	LXXX	1000	M
7	VII	17	XVII	90	XC	1500	MD
8	VIII	18	XVIII	100	C	2000	MM
9	IX	19	XIX	200	CC	5000	$\overline{V}$
10	X	20	XX	300	CCC	1,000,000	$\overline{M}$

1800	MDCCC
1920	MCMXX
1755	MDCCLV

1. Use of Roman numerals:

Henry VIII   John Astor III   Chapter XI

2. When writing a series of Roman numerals, leave an extra space after each comma:

Volumes X, XII, XX, XXV

EXERCISE

Type the following sentences, making all necessary corrections:

1. There were three offices on the 4th floor of the six story building.
2. 42 men applied for the job that paid six thousand dollars a year.
3. The train will arrive between 4 and 5 o'clock on April 18th.
4. They bought two nine by twelve foot rugs and paid $350.00 for them.
5. His policy (number 12,385) for ten thousand dollars has expired.
6. One hundred and thirty two men boarded the train at two a. m.
7. The table she purchased measures 3¼ by 5 3/4 feet.
8. The work was ¼ finished when the eighteen women arrived today.

Lesson 12

EXERCISE 10 — ALPHABETIC SENTENCES

The lazy boy worked diligently because he expected me to give him a quart jar of fresh milk.

Just before dawn, an extremely thick haze spread quickly over the peacefully sleeping village.

Jill was amazed at the sight of so many exquisite birds provided by the city for the zoo in the park.

EXERCISE 11 — BALANCED HAND DRILL

the for rug but did she bit and due got end she fit eye cot
man dot lap bug hen own oak pry nap men ham pen pal hem cot
also city duty envy fork girl held lamb make name when paid
right blame risks firms spent shape usual widow chair gowns
ancient bicycle dismal emblem thrown visible haughty neighs

EXERCISE 12 — DOUBLE LETTER DRILL

sob sobbing ace access mad madder made fled fleet oft offered
gag gagged real really coma comma wind winner fun funny funds
chose choose chosen sup supper bare barred mast amass process
antic attic butt butler size sizzled babble succeed supported
oddity career bluffs goggle wholly mummy winning voodoo apple

PARAGRAPH STRESSING DOUBLE LETTERS

Needless to say, I am happy for the opportunity to cooperate 59
with you in the planning of the new office for the bookkeeping 120
department of the Hall Lumber Company. Our staff has suggested 182
a green pattern for the wall to match the floor matting in the 243
office, but I can discuss this fully with you when we meet next 305
week. It will be unnecessary for you to supply a summary of all 368
the work done because I will have little occasion to refer to it. 432
However, the comments you made referring to the material that 492
will be needed have been helpful, and I will be able to make good 556
use of this additional information. 590

REFERENCE CHART

AGE	Spell out an age stated in years. Use figures for an age that includes months and days. Omit commas between the years, months, and days.	I am eighteen. I am 18 years 4 months and 27 days old.
DATES	Use figures except in extremely formal documents. Use -st, -nd, -rd, -th in a date *only* when the day is written before the month. The year may be abbreviated by using an apostrophe for the century.	August 6, 19— the 6th of August Class of '61 the blizzard of '88
DIMENSIONS FEET INCHES WEIGHTS DISTANCE	Use figures for dimensions. In technical material, use the apostrophe (') to represent feet, and quotation marks (") to represent inches. Do not space between the number and mark. Note use of number sign (#) for pounds.	4 by 6 feet 4' x 6' 4 feet 6 inches 4'6" 6 lbs. 6# 3 miles
LEGAL DOCUMENTS	At one time, numbers were spelled out, followed by the figure in parentheses. Modern practice tends toward the use of figures only.	We agree to sell thirty-three (33) acres. We agree to sell 33 acres.
MONEY	Use figures, except in extremely formal legal documents. Do not space after the dollar sign. Omit the decimal point and ciphers for even amounts (except in checks or in a series that contains an uneven amount). For amounts under $1, use the cent sign (¢) only in invoices, etc.	$12.73 $8.05 $12 $3.45 list, $3.00 net 4 @ 8¢ We paid 8 cents
PERCENTAGES	Use figures to express percentages. Percent may be written as one word or as two. Use the percentage sign (%) only in business forms and statistical work. Do not space before the percentage sign.	12 percent 12 per cent 12%
REFERENCE NUMBERS	Use figures for reference numbers that identify a model, style, policy, invoice, purchase order, page, volume, etc. Generally omit all commas in such numbers. Common nouns, such as model or chapter, should be capitalized when used before reference numbers.	Model #23546 Policy No. S98467 Invoice 20741 Chapter 7 Lesson III Room 2
TIME	Spell out the hour with o'clock. Use figures with a.m. and p.m. Either lower case or capital letters may be used. Do not space after *a.* or *p.* Use a colon to separate hours from minutes and minutes from seconds.	four o'clock 4 a.m. 4:03 P.M. 4:03:26

Lesson 13

EXERCISE 13   ALPHABETIC SENTENCES

The audience enjoyed the meeting, but some of them were puzzled by the queer views expounded by the speaker.

Many express trains that were bound for the city whizzed down the tracks along the jagged bank of the quiet river.

They judged it very unwise to minimize the danger of his plight because he knew what to expect.

Jack was extremely awkward on the stage, but he fought back the impulsive urge to quit.

EXERCISE 14   CAPITAL LETTER DRILL

All Alas Bit Both Cod Cure Dog Dumb Eye Else For Firm God Guns
Hat Helm Ire Item Jay Jest Key Kate Let Lake Met Mate Net Navy
Ore Oath Pay Pat Pest Quit Rod Rust Sun Some Tub Told Use Ural
Vie Voted Won With Yes Year Zoo Zoom Anita Jack Doris Lawrence
England Iran Peru Spanish Ireland China Jamaica Dutch Japanese

EXERCISE 15   E AND I DRILL

irk end ion end icy end imp end ire end ice end ivy end its end
eye did eel did eke did ear did eat did eve did elm did ebb did
lie item lied iris lied iron lied idle lied iced lied itch lied
vie let lit hem him wit wet led lid peg pig mere mire fell fill
fired beige crier siege being reign piers weighed priest pieced

PARAGRAPH STRESSING E AND I

This is the time for you to think of a winter suit for your   63
little girl. If you wait until the end of the month, you will   125
find that the wide choice available now is gone and you will be   188
very limited in your selection. We invite you to visit our new   251
store during the coming week to see our varied stock. I am sure   315
that you will see a line of suits to delight the heart of every   378
fashion-minded young miss. We will be here to welcome you and   440
serve your needs.   457

5. Form the plural of a figure by adding an apostrophe followed by the letter s ('s). If a number is spelled out, just add the letter **s**.

        8's and 9's
        eights and nines
        1900's

DECIMALS

1. A period is used to express a decimal point. Do not skip a space before or after the period.

        1.06   12.412   128.627

2. Do not use commas in the decimal part of a number.

            1.08
          47.62432
        2,974.4216

FRACTIONS

There are two kinds of typewritten fractions—those that are on the keyboard ($\frac{1}{2}$) and those that are made by using the diagonal (1/19). Note that there is no space before or after the diagonal.

1. Use figures for all mixed numbers. With a keyboard fraction, no space is left between the whole number and the fraction. With a "made" fraction, one space is left.

        $2\frac{1}{2}$ 2 5/16
        $4\frac{1}{4}$ 18 4/100

2. Do not use a "typewriter-key fraction" ($\frac{1}{2}$) in the same sentence with a "made" fraction (1/8).

        The lot measures 84 1/2 by 26 1/8 feet.
        NOT: The lot measures $84\frac{1}{2}$ by 26 1/8 feet.

3. Spell out all isolated fractions. Generally, hyphenate such a fraction.

        The job is two-thirds completed.
        Asphalt was used for four-tenths of a mile.

66

Lesson 14

EXERCISE 16   ALPHABETIC SENTENCES

```
        I know that the junior squad was expected to give a new
horizontal bar for the school gym.

        Many were dazzled by the sight of the exquisitely fine
jewels which sparkled on the shelves.

        They wanted the quartet to begin their evening program by
harmonizing ballads from the back country.
```

EXERCISE 17   FIRST FINGER DRILL

```
gap fill gay fill get fill gem fill got fill guy fill gum fill
tag fled tap fled the fled two fled try fled too fled ton fled
has jump had jump hay jump her jump his jump him jump how jump
you jars yes jars yet jars your jars yell jars yoke jars years
bad file bag file bat file ban file bed file bet file bog file
```

EXERCISE 18   FIRST FINGER DRILL

```
fad rang fat rang far rang few rang for rang fur rang fun rang
rap fold ran fold red fold rib fold rig fold rib fold rip fold
vat funk vex funk vane funk vice funk vile funk vote funk vest
nap jack not jack nor jack now jack nod jack net jack new jack
tame join most join norm join myth join navy joins muted joins
```

PARAGRAPH STRESSING FIRST FINGER

We were very glad to get such a fine order from you for	54
several copies of our valuable new book. If you want us to send	117
them to you in one big package, just let us know. I can promise	180
that the shipment will go out to you at once. It is our opinion	243
that this is the best book of its type to be published in many	304
years, and I am certain that you will find it valuable for	361
teaching your students better English. A number of important	421
people have already voiced their approval of this book and once	483
you have used it, I feel sure you will agree with them.	537

HYPHENATING SPELLED-OUT NUMBERS

1. Hyphenate spelled-out numbers from twenty-one through ninety-nine.

        Twenty-one
        Forty-six
        Ninety-nine

2. Do not hyphenate before the words *hundred, thousand,* etc. (Note: The *and* may be omitted.)

        One hundred and twenty-one
        One thousand three hundred forty-six
        Seventy-six thousand four hundred and ninety-nine

WRITING FIGURES

1. Figures from 1 to 1000 are written without commas.

        2   932
        32   1000

2. Figures above 1000 are generally written with commas to separate every three digits. This permits ease of reading. Leave no space before or after the comma.

        1,001   1,426
        1,932   7,320

3. Below 10,000 you may omit the commas from numbers rounded out to the nearest hundred; above 10,000, the comma must be included.

        1100   1,101   10,000
        5200   5,274   10,100
        9900   9,999   23,500

4. When two figures appear one after the other, separate them by a comma. Skip a space after the comma.

        Of 1700, 23 were rejected.

Lesson 15

In typing the following drills, remember to space **once** after a comma or a semicolon and **twice** after a colon, a question mark, or a period. There is one space after a period only when it **occurs** after an abbreviation. (For example: *Mr. Brown*)

EXERCISE 19   PUNCTUATION DRILL

```
She is ill.  Do not yell.  She can call.  See the white sail.
They fail.  Your doll.  Old mill.  Their mail.  Mr. T. Small.
you look, can talk, lack, take back, deep dark, break, brick,
Be still.  Yes, it is.  No, not me.  Oh, I know.  True, I am.
```

EXERCISE 20   PUNCTUATION DRILL

```
    Here is the bill.  It is hers.  Give it to me.  It is not
mine.  Ask her for it.  Please do it now.  This is the one.

    Give me the book, pen, and the ink.  I sold the balls to
Mary, Jane, and Jack; of course, they all paid for them.

    All work, so they say, is bad.  At last, we are at home.
Yes, I have it.  She bought yellow, black, and green paint.

    No more; until tomorrow; as of now; please wait; if not;
Did you?  May we?  Can they tell?  Is it here?  Are they not?
This list:  the following:  as given:  Here are all the facts:
```

EXERCISE 21   PUNCTUATION DRILL

```
    By doing, not saying, it is done.  Say what you will, the
pen, the pencil, and the box are gone.  Will you find them?

    All, not part, is required.  Does he want eight, nine, or
ten?  You may, if you must, leave now.  Are you ready to go?

    Helen, not Mary, cooked breakfast, lunch, and dinner for
us.  If, when I come, you have not arrived, I will not wait.

    Did you, while at home, read the book?  If not, then take
it now.  Oh, did you say you bought a copy?  Where is it?
```

Lesson 39

RULES FOR TYPING NUMBERS

WHEN TO SPELL OUT NUMBERS AND WHEN TO USE FIGURES

1. Spell out whole numbers from one through ten. Use figures above ten.

> We sent four packages.
> He received ten letters.
> They ordered 11 sets of books.
> This mailing consisted of 10,000 letters.

2. Spell out numbers that begin a sentence, no matter how large. (When a long number begins a sentence, it is often better to rearrange the sentence.)

> Two hundred twenty-eight men applied for the job.
> The job was applied for by 228 men.

3. Generally spell out approximate numbers that have been rounded out.

> About three hundred men applied for the job.

4. Ordinal numbers are "first," "second," "third," etc. Spell out ordinal numbers from *first* through *tenth*. Use figures for *11th* and above.

> This is my fourth visit to your city.
> He succeeded on the 11th attempt.
> This is my 25th crossing.

5. When two numbers appear one after the other, spell out the smaller number and express the larger number in figures. This prevents confusion.

> The purchasing department ordered eleven 55-gallon drums.
> We need 11 three-cent stamps.

6. Use figures in all statistical typing and tabulation, and in all business forms.

> 4 cartons   No. 10 envelopes
> 3 boxes   8" x 10" letterheads
> 12 cartons   3" x 5" index cards

7. When a series of numbers includes numbers both above and below ten, use figures for all the numbers.

> We ordered 8 boxes of paper, 12 boxes of envelopes,
> and 20 cartons of index cards.

Lesson 16

EXERCISE 22   **ALPHABETIC SENTENCES**

After a very exciting day, the boy came home, took out a jigsaw puzzle and played quietly until bedtime.

The citizens requested the government official to make the topic of Social Security the subject of his next talk.

Dazed and exhausted by his victory, the prize fighter came from the ring and walked quickly through the jostling crowd.

EXERCISE 23   **FIRST ROW DRILL**

crop dice camp dice cute dice city dice clue dice code dice card
exile next annex next flaxy next oxide next waxen next taxi next
waltz plaza zonal plaza sized plaza graze plaza zebra plaza zest
savor verbs river verbs liver verbs rover verbs favor verbs hive
clove drive clove brace clove exits clove grave clove exalt barb

EXERCISE 24   **SENTENCES STRESSING FIRST ROW**

Before she drove away, did she give explicit directions concerning the exact size of the chintz couch cover?

We expect the five prizes to be given to the contestants after the election committee has announced its choice.

The teacher explained each exercise to her puzzled class; then they realized the benefits to be derived from them.

EXERCISE 25   **FIRST, SECOND AND THIRD ROW DRILL**

asks sad lads salad flasks glass had falls half glad shall dash
quiet were route true your power quote worry riot pet purr quit
box man numb came lax size mane coax vice amaze lamb many above
exit bomb crumb couch mummy stumble section enzyme wizen number
8 men, 6 new pens, 34 brave boys, 16 names, 15 votes, 93 cloaks

HALF-SPACE METHOD (Continued)

To *eliminate* an unnecessary letter with the half-space method:

    Example: Tell them about it.   (Change *them* to *her*.)

1. Erase the entire word that is to be corrected—*them*.
2. Move carriage to where the first letter had been. (In this example, move carriage to the original "*t*" position.)
3. Depress the space bar and, *while the space bar is depressed,* strike the first letter of the correct word. (In this example, strike "*h*.")
4. Release the space bar and depress it again for the insertion of the second letter (*e*). Continue in this way until the third letter has been inserted.

    Result: Tell her about it.

BACKSPACE METHOD

For machines that do not half-space, use the following methods to insert or delete letters.

1. Erase the entire word that is being corrected.
2. Move the carriage to where the *first* letter of the original word had been.
3. To *insert* a single letter, space *once* . . . To *delete* a single letter, space *twice* . . . and then *fully* depress the backspace key. Keeping it depressed, strike the first letter of the word that is to be inserted.
4. Release the backspace key and space once. Depress the backspace key again and, *while it is depressed,* insert the next letter.
5. Release the backspace key and repeat Step 4 until the entire word has been corrected.

EXERCISE

First type each of the following sentences, disregarding the words in parentheses. Then correct the sentences to include the words in parentheses in place of the underscored words.

Practice on each sentence until you can make a neat correction before proceeding to the next sentence.

1. We received your <u>bills</u> (bill) on <u>Monday</u> (Tuesday) morning.
2. The order <u>will</u> (may) be ready <u>next</u> (about) Monday.
3. Your <u>check</u> (bill) to us <u>wasn't</u> (was not) received.
4. We <u>spoke</u> (talked) about our <u>visit</u> (trip) to the plant.
5. There were <u>seven</u> (five) men and <u>six</u> (four) women present.

63

Lesson 17

EXERCISE 26   ALPHABETIC SENTENCES

Six years of valuable experience should qualify him to
judge whether Jack deserves the prize.

At her job, the lazy girl was required to check all tax
forms and then give them to her employer for signature.

A bronze plaque was given to the jockey to commemorate
the extremely fine record he had established.

EXERCISE 27   DIFFICULT STROKE DRILL

cry arch acts itch aces echo duct acre fact cede march witches
hum imp mops myth hump come smog mules thumb hymn pomp minimum
inn nut ton not any find snip anon into fund noun inning nymph
very even verve give have carve level clever serve starve ever
bed ebb able baby debt bath obey rebel curbs barber about barn
boy sly spy myth many your funny pygmy ably ally style bicycle

EXERCISE 28   FOURTH FINGER DRILL

all pulp ask pulp ash pulp add pulp aid pulp air pulp are pulp
age quiz and quiz any quiz aye quiz ape quiz act quiz ace quiz
zoo ails zip ails zeal ails zest ails zero ails zinc ails zoom
pay load pan load pet load pew load put load pig load pin load
all quip awl quip army quip also quip away quip aide quip able

PARAGRAPH STRESSING FOURTH FINGER

Your inquiry about our custom-fitted sport coats and suits	57
is appreciated. The quality of our materials and the equipment	119
that we use in our workshops assure you that a suit purchased	179
from us will fit properly and give you years of continuous	236
service. We point with pride to the long list of customers who	298
return to us year after year; we are sure that you will be	355
equally pleased and will buy many suits from us in the future.	415
We carry a complete stock in all sizes and there are dozens of	477
styles from which you can choose.	509

ERASING CARBON COPIES

When erasing an original letter with one or more carbon copies, the general steps outlined on the previous page must be supplemented by the following:

1. Before making the erasure, insert a *stiff* card *immediately* behind the spot where the correction is to be made. Doing this will prevent the pressure used in erasing from smudging the other copies. After each correction is made, remove the card and place it behind the next copy to be erased.

2. Use a hard eraser on the original copy and a soft eraser for correcting carbon copies. Make certain the eraser is clean before attempting to make a correction with it.

3. To darken a carbon correction after erasing, set the ribbon control lever in stencil position and firmly type over the original copy.

SQUEEZING AND EXPANDING

HALF-SPACE METHOD

Errors resulting from the insertion or omission of a single letter or space can be corrected by a method known as "half-spacing." This method takes advantage of the fact that the space bar on most typewriters moves the carriage forward in two half-space movements—one half space when the bar is depressed and another half space when the bar is released. Thus, by properly operating the space bar it is possible to insert or delete extra letters by increasing or decreasing the *space between words* by a half space.

To check your machine for half-spacing, press down on the space bar and then release it. If the carriage moved twice—both when you depressed the bar and when you released it—you may use the following method for the insertion of an omitted letter. If it moved only once, you must use the backspace method explained on the next page.

To *insert* a single letter with the half-space method:

Example: They se the typewriter.   (*se*, instead of *see*)

1. Erase the entire word that is to be corrected. (In this example, erase *se*.)
2. Move the carriage to the space *after* the previous word. (In this example, move the carriage to the space after *they*.)
3. Depress the space bar (this moves the carriage a half space) and, *keeping the space bar in a depressed position,* type the first letter of the corrected word. (In this example, strike "*s*.")
4. Release the space bar and depress it again and, *while the space bar is depressed,* strike the second letter (*e*) of the word that is being corrected. Continue in this way until the third letter has been inserted. Remember—the space bar must be in the depressed position while each letter is being inserted.

Result: They see the typewriter.

Lesson 18

EXERCISE 29   SENTENCES STRESSING E AND I

From the pier they perceived a derelict ship being carried
to the shore by the high tide.

I believe that she has the ability to write an effective
and entertaining business letter.

Their neighbor spent his leisure time either at picnics
near the beach or on hikes to distant fields.

EXERCISE 30   SECOND FINGER DRILL

```
day kill did kill die kill dip kill dig kill dim kill dew
ere deal ear deal eat deal end deal eel deal eke deal eve
can dirk car dirk cat dirk cap dirk cod dirk cow dirk cup
kid desk kin desk kit desk key desk kind desk king desk
its kink ill kink ink kink ice kink ivy kink ire kink irk
cab dark cad dark can dark cop dark cot dark cud dark card
```

EXERCISE 31   THIRD FINGER DRILL

```
led sway lap sway leg sway lug sway let sway log sway lad sway
sad exit sew exit sip exit saw exit sat exit son exit set exit
was slow win slow wax slow wit slow way slow wet slow won slow
oar lull odd lull off lull one lull own lull oil lull ore lull
lax seal lax sled lax salt lax slow lax soul lax slot lax sill
```

PARAGRAPH STRESSING SECOND AND THIRD FINGERS

While we wish it were possible for us to fill your recent   56
order, we cannot do so until we are in receipt of a check from   117
you. We realize that business has been extremely slow in your   178
county, and we were willing to wait until you could settle your   240
account. Six months have now passed, however, since we last   299
heard from you in regard to this matter, and unless we receive   360
word from you within the next week, we will be obliged to refuse   422
your order.   432

ERASING

Accurate typing is the goal of every typist. The most experienced typist, however, will occasionally make an error, and it is, therefore, essential to learn the proper methods for correcting these mistakes.

If you must erase an error, follow these steps so as to avoid the necessity of retyping the letter completely:

1. Move the carriage to either the left or the right past the margin stops, so that the erasure particles will not drop into the "well" or basket of the machine and clog the keys.
2. Raise the paper bail out of the way.

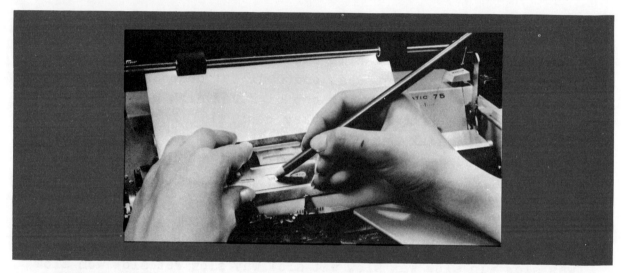

3. If the correction is to be made on the upper two-thirds of the page, turn the paper up to a convenient position. If the correction is to be made on the lower part of the page, turn the cylinder backward so as not to disturb the alignment of the typing line.
4. Use an eraser shield to protect the letters surrounding the one to be corrected. These shields, made either of metal, paper, or celluloid, are perforated in such a way that the perforations can be placed over the letters to be corrected thus avoiding any unintentional erasing of the letters around it.
5. Proper erasing technique requires a *light*, short, downward stroke. Do not "scrub" or you will suddenly find a hole in your paper. Using a clean eraser, stroke downward lightly. Examine your progress after each stroke of the eraser. The trick is to erase as *little* as possible. When the erasure is complete, blow any erasure crumbs off the page or typewriter.
6. Return the carriage to the proper position and *lightly* strike the correct letter. Backspace, and strike it *lightly* again, continuing this process until the correction is as dark as the surrounding type. If you have neatly and carefully followed these steps, your erasure will not be noticed.

(CONTINUED ON NEXT PAGE)

Lesson 19

EXERCISE 32   ALPHABETIC SENTENCES

When I realized that my fur jacket was exceptionally tight and quite beyond repair, I gave it to her.

Just when her bookkeeping average was extremely high, my friend, Hazel, was forced to quit school.

The angry boy jumped up and seized his ax when he saw the squealing pigs chewing the vegetables in back of the house.

EXERCISE 33   ADJACENT STROKE DRILL

far fat mar mat try raft tart bear beat rates trait rattlers
saw eat law ear wet owe eve draw ewer brew went sewed wealth
sly use buy yet yule ably ugly only urges unity usual yearly
aft age safe sage flag flog fate gate graft golf grief fling
add dads lads dish beds soda dear dress desk skids addresses
red her met tree never earn serve earth bare real gear gender

EXERCISE 34   K-L DRILL

larks sale larks sake larks silk larks sill larks soil larks
keep liked keys liked king liked knew liked know liked kneel
lady faked laid faked land faked lest faked lead faked lakes
large flask laugh flask leads flask least flask learn flask
kilts black lucky black plank black skill black walks black

PARAGRAPH STRESSING K AND L

If you will take just a moment to look at the back cover of   58
our booklet, you will be able to read the names of the local   117
stores in New York that handle our bakery products. As you may   178
know, we make all our cakes and cookies from fresh milk and eggs.   242
Also, the bakers who work in our plant have all had long years of   306
experience in this field. Mail the card that is enclosed and we   369
will call at the end of the week to take your order.   420

41

CARBON COPIES

It is customary to make a carbon copy of every letter or form that is typed in a business office. The number of copies required will depend upon the procedures followed by the organization. As a general rule, at least one carbon copy will be made and kept in the company files.

Carbon copies of business letters are never typed on letterhead stationery. Instead, a blank sheet (generally inexpensive yellow paper or onionskin) is used. Carbon copies of business forms—such as invoices or statements—are typed on printed forms similar to the original.

Notice that there is a dull side and a glossy side to a sheet of carbon paper. (See illustration.) It is the glossy side that prints. Therefore, the glossy side is placed *against* the sheet on which the carbon copy is to be made.

To prepare your paper for insertion into the machine:

1. Lay the paper to be used for the carbon copy on your desk. Place the carbon paper over it, with the glossy side down.

2. On top of these sheets, place the letterhead, face up. Note in the illustration the arrangement for an original and two copies.

3. Place the sheets in position for insertion with the printed letterhead resting against the paper table.

4. Check for the proper arrangement of the carbon paper by making sure that its glossy side faces you as the papers are being inserted behind the cylinder.

5. Insert the papers.

6. When it is necessary to insert a thick pack of several sheets into the machine, the sheets may be kept in alignment during insertion by placing a folded piece of paper, or the flap of an envelope, over the top of the sheets. (See illustration)

For erasing carbon copies, see page 62.

Lesson 20

EXERCISE 35   ALPHABETIC SENTENCES

Jack, in a quiet voice said, "By fighting a war, man may well expect to destroy his civilization."

The very dazed explorer, wandering by chance in the quiet jungle, found tusks of many elephants--their burial ground.

Sixty blazing fires were started by the earthquake that completely ruined the Javanese city. Hundreds were injured.

EXERCISE 36   PICA: 15-71   ELITE: 23-79   THIRD FINGER DRILL

```
lean kilns line kilns loan kilns lost kilns lute kilns
sale doled safe doled said doled sell doled seen doled
some scold soon scold side scold sign scold sure scold
wall seals wait seals what seals when seals whom seals
well sells were sells went sells will sells wish sells
xyst soled axle soled axes soled exit soled coax soled
```

EXERCISE 37   FOURTH FINGER DRILL

```
quay asked quart asked quiz asked quit asked quip asked quote
zany sails zone sails zest sails zero sails zeal sails zodiac
place fools pride fools point fools proper fools papers fools
quiet aches quite aches quest aches queer aches quickly aches
added quilt again quilt after quilt about quilt above quilted
pass piles page piles pipe piles past piles pole piles prompt
```

PARAGRAPH STRESSING THIRD AND FOURTH FINGER

Two weeks ago, at your request, we forwarded an itemized statement of your account showing the balance due. We have had no word from you since. We wish it were within our power to extend the date of payment, but it is the policy of this company not to relax its rules in such matters. We must therefore urge you to pay the balance at once. We realize the difficulties you have encountered, but we feel that we have been quite fair in allowing you sixty days in which to make payment. We are extremely sorry that we cannot give you the extra time you requested.

55
117
176
239
301
364
424
480
537
546

RULES FOR CAPITALIZATION

The following are the most important rules governing the capitalization of words. You should use a capital letter for:

1. The first word in a sentence.

    Send it to them now.

2. A proper name or a derivative from a proper name.

    John Smith   America   American

3. A noun that is part of the name of a *specific* product, geographical location, hotel, highway, etc.

    The best fan is the Arctic Fan.
    The Mississippi River is the longest river in America.
    The finest hotel is the Hotel Sands.

4. The title of a person when it appears *directly* before or after the name of the title-holder. There is some disagreement about whether the title of a person should be capitalized when his name does not appear in a sentence. The preferred business practice is to capitalize such titles, especially the title of high-ranking officers. After all, you express your respect for a person when you capitalize his title.

    Send the message to John Johnson, President of the Acme Steel
    Company.
    The Sales Manager called the meeting to order.
    BUT: Do you know who is the sales manager of the Ajax Company?

5. The name of a point on the compass when it refers to a specific geographical area, but **NOT** when it refers to a direction.

    The West is less populated than those areas east of the Mississippi.

6. The name of a month or a day, but NOT of a season.

    The first day of spring will be Tuesday, March 21.

7. Each word in the title of a work of art or literature, except prepositions, conjunctions, and articles. However, the first word is *always* capitalized.

    Have you read "How to Win Friends and Influence People"?

8. The first word in a direct quotation that starts a complete sentence.

    "This job," he said, "must be improved upon."

9. A noun or pronoun that refers to God or specific holy books.

    In the Bible we are told that God created the world in six
    days and that He rested on the seventh day.

Lesson 21

EXERCISE 38   ALPHABETIC SENTENCES

The junior executive requested an itemized account of all expenses during the trip from New York to Baltimore.

The officer quizzed the taxi driver who, in attempting to avoid injuring the boy, had driven his cab on the sidewalk.

From the back porch, I could see the extremely lovely sight of the yellow jonquils swaying in the morning breeze.

EXERCISE 39   U-O-I DRILL

usage joins usual joins under joins unite joins utter joins
idler ducks idiom ducks inner ducks inter ducks issue ducks
loads union local union limit union occur union ideal union
toils likes coils likes foils likes soils likes boils likes
house point youth point touch point rough point mouse point

EXERCISE 40   ALPHABETIC REVIEW

was greed panels hopes colleges onyx pare miracles able father
botanical square breakers begin crazed rightly joker hopefully
jaunts milk vines bottles human myself flames melting brakeman
winning impel cathedrals idioms mutually cloak causeless prize
frenzy melted limiting jerks taxicab comfortless carats stoops

PARAGRAPH STRESSING ALPHABET REVIEW

As requested in your letter, we are enclosing a folder	53
giving the rates at our hotel for the months of June and July.	114
Now that summer is coming, many people are beginning to make	173
plans to leave the city for week-ends and vacations. We expect	234
that the rooms which are now available will be quickly rented.	295
We know that you will like it here. Every room was designed and	358
equipped by experts to insure that you will be comfortable during	422
your stay. The six experienced cooks in our kitchen special-	484
ize in preparing food that will certainly please and delight	544
you. Make your reservations in advance.	584

43

7. Divide words only between syllables. However, do not divide a word in such a way that a single letter is separated from the remainder of the word. (If you are in doubt as to the proper syllabication of a word, take the time to consult your dictionary.)

Correct:		Incorrect:	
con-tain			e-lated
trans-fer			a-mong
edu-cates			radi-o
con-di-tion			o-blige

8. Divide compound words only at the point where the hyphen occurs.

sister-in-law   self-control   above-mentioned

9. As a general rule, divide words between double letters unless the word is derived from one that ends in a double letter (sma*ll*). In the latter case, the word is divided after the root word.

small-est   rub-ber
woo-ing   excel-lence
stuff-ing   win-ning

Remember—When in doubt, consult the dictionary.

EXERCISE

Where would you divide the words in the following list? **In those** words that *can* be divided, use a hyphen to indicate the proper syllabication. If the word *cannot* be divided, type it without hyphenating.

Example: con-tin-u-a-tion   edu-cates   enough

shipment	maintained	tallest
develop	modernized	against
unnecessary	first-rate	constitution
departing	percentage	regardless
along	margins	evaluate
running	every	stenography
filling	stopped	secretary
electric	procedure	wouldn't
sentence	performance	salutation
followed	typewriting	upon

Lesson 22

EXERCISE 41   ALPHABETIC SENTENCES

Dazed and frightened, the quivering boys limped to join
the crowd of shrieking citizens.

The impoverished quartet finally signed a contract to play
with the newly-organized jazz band.

The red fox jumped over the wall as the very excited man
came into view brandishing a shotgun.

EXERCISE 42   LEFT AND RIGHT HAND DRILL

sad bat wet bad are cab far saw was red bar few wax tar rat gas
lip pin you him joy hop nip kin oil ply hum ill mop ink hip inn
gave data ears wage read tact brew vast acre seat care face dad
jump milk hymn lily mink kill yolk pulp kiln moon polo hump pun
tasted onion braved milky drafted union swear pupil cadet imply

EXERCISE 43   BV-MN DRILL

vain fiber very fiber vast fiber veto fiber vale fiber vote
bark favor born favor bury favor bomb favor bone favor boat
nail jumpy name jumpy near jumpy nest jumpy need jumpy nose
made jails must jails make jails more jails meet jails main
noun jests many jests mine jests norm jests navy jests moan

PARAGRAPH STRESSING BV AND MN

Our records indicate the fact that we have not received an   57
order from your company in recent months. Have you had cause to 120
find fault with our stock or our service? If such is the case, I 184
would consider it a favor if you would be kind enough to mail a 246
note to me informing me what we have done to displease you. I am 310
sure that whatever the difficulty might be, it can be ironed out 373
promptly. Because we have always looked on you as one of our   433
most valuable customers, I hope to have word from you within a   494
very short time.   509

MAINTAINING THE RIGHT-HAND MARGIN

In typing unarranged copy, it will be necessary for you to decide where to end each line in order to maintain a reasonably straight right-hand margin.

The bell on your typewriter will serve to warn you that six or eight strokes may be typed before the carriage locks against the right margin. Thus, as you type, listen for the sound of the bell. When you hear it, finish the word you are typing—if it is not too long—and throw your carriage without taking your eyes from your copy.

If typing only two or three strokes beyond the margin will permit you to complete the word, strike the margin release when the carriage locks at the margin and insert these extra letters. However, if the word you are typing is too long for your line of type, divide it properly as explained below, and continue the word on the next line.

WORD DIVISION

The trend in letter writing today is to avoid the use of word divisions whenever possible. Therefore, the guiding rule of every typist should be to divide words only when it is absolutely necessary to do so in order to maintain a *reasonably* straight right margin. A line of type that is five spaces shorter than the margin or three spaces longer is acceptable in business practice.

Learn the following rules before you type any unarranged copy:

1. When dividing a word, the hyphen should be typed at the end of the first line—never at the beginning of the second.

2. Do not divide a proper noun, a contraction, an abbreviation, or a number.

3. If possible, do not divide a word if it is the last word of a paragraph or a page.

4. Do not end more than two successive lines with a divided word.

5. Do not divide a one-syllable word or a word of less than five letters.

```
        where           please          talked
        think           through         shipped
```

6. Carry over at least three or more letters.

```
Correct:    shortly              Incorrect:    short-ly
            lux-ury                            luxu-ry
            con-sumer                          consum-er
```

Lesson 23

EXERCISE 44   ALPHABETIC SENTENCES

The woman quickly sealed the five dozen glass jars of strawberry preserves with wax.

The foreman was expecting delivery of benzene and liquid glue by the first week in January.

Sixty zebras were brought back by the museum's well-equipped expedition into the African jungle.

EXERCISE 45   FIRST FINGER DRILL

```
your judge yarn judge yawn judge yard judge year judge yell
half jells have jells hurt jells hand jells here jells high
band favor brag favor bury favor back favor bolt favor bias
bear verbs best verbs burr verbs bite verbs bent verbs both
fade gulfs face gulfs fact gulfs feed gulfs fine gulfs form
```

EXERCISE 46   FIRST FINGER DRILL

```
flag raft film raft fire raft firm raft five raft from raft
main jumps many jumps name jumps mint jumps noun jumps mine
vast brave vane brave vary brave very brave vine brave vile
jail usury jolt usury joke usury join usury just usury jury
used fjord ugly fjord upon fjord undo fjord unit fjord unto
```

PARAGRAPH STRESSING FIRST FINGER

During the last week of November, our store is going to move 59
from its present location on Main Street to Broadway. For this 121
reason, we are going to hold our annual leather and luggage sale 184
at an early date. We are, therefore, sending you this invitation 249
to inspect our stock of beautiful traveling bags. Every item in 312
our large department is going to be drastically reduced and we 373
know that you will be able to obtain valuable leather pieces at 435
bargain rates. We want our charge-account customers to have 494
first choice, so come in soon. 523

Lesson 34

ALPHABET DRILLS (*Continued*)

Y | yes yet you your youth yacht yard yeast yoke you've yellow younger

Everybody displayed great sympathy for the unhappy gypsy leader.
Were they angry with you yesterday for taking the bicycle away?

     In reply to your inquiry, I am sorry to say that our factory
cannot possibly supply the quantity of yellow party frocks that are
necessary to fill your order. As I told you in my conversation
yesterday, the holiday season is always a very busy one, and our
supply of the style and quality you desire is quickly depleted by
orders from all over the country. I hope the twenty dresses that
went out to you today will prove satisfactory in every way.

Z | zoo zinc zeal zero zest zone zebra zircon zipper zealous zoology

A dozen citizens analyzed the report but each was puzzled by it.
Freezing rain made the zigzag trail to the summit very hazardous.

     The size of your overdue account is a small one and we are
puzzled and amazed to find that you have not paid it. Of course,
we realize that conditions have been bad and we recognize the fact
that your organization was unable to utilize its equipment during
the freezing weather. However, I must again emphasize that unless
we hear from you, we will be forced to bring suit against you.

Lesson 24

EXERCISE 47   **ALPHABETIC SENTENCES**

The six squads of weary men climbed into the jeeps and drove back to camp through the freezing rain.

After having heard the lawyer's eloquent plea, the jury retired to a back room to analyze the perplexing case.

Queen Elizabeth, wearing her famous jewels, went very slowly to the ship and extended her hand to the captain.

EXERCISE 48   **DK-SL SUBSTITUTION DRILL**

sale list slam list salt list sole list soil list slur list seal
song long sure lure sift lift sunk lung sate late silt lilt sulk
king duck know duck keys duck knit duck kick duck kill duck kind
keen desk kiss desk kind desk knot desk knew desk kept desk kept
leak lock lack lock luck lock link lock lark lock lake lock look

EXERCISE 49   **ALPHABETIC REVIEW**

shaken dealers manly muscles sized cancellation usage misplace
whenever equips clatters college rocker everyone contemptibles
managing thank beautiful page approval zinc sentimentally jaws
thrown cancels gravy sixfold beginning croaked halters cruller
left chuckle peeking controlling failure manifold flaming wish
jovial flaxen taken couple racing equally replied imperial six

PARAGRAPH STRESSING ALPHABET REVIEW

This is just a note to tell you that we thank you very much   58
for giving us your insurance business. The policy which we are   120
enclosing is evidence of the great protection and savings that   180
will be made available to you. We suggest that you read it with   243
extreme care to make sure that it is written just exactly as you   306
wish. If you should have any questions that you would like to   367
ask, do not hesitate to acquaint us with them. We are here to   428
serve you. Be assured that our interest does not depend upon the   492
size of your policy.   511

Lesson 33

ALPHABET DRILLS (Continued)

V | very vary view vote veto value visit vile vain verb vine voltage

They covered every heavy vase with velvet before having it moved.
Everyone who served gave their vote in favor of paving the avenue.

Please give us the chance to help you solve whatever problem
you have in moving to your new home. Every piece of furniture
will be carefully covered to avoid damage; all valuable silverware
will be wrapped in velvet to prevent scratching. The drivers of
our moving vans are each heavily insured and your moving job will
be over in four or five hours.

W | was way who why want week what when with whom will well wish went

Were you with the woman when she went down to buy the yellow gown?
The crowd viewed the showing of the crown jewels with silent awe.

The letter you wrote was left on my desk when I had gone away
for a week and did not reach me until now. I checked with our
foreman and learned that the watch which you forwarded to us for
repair was sent out by Railway Express on Wednesday, and it should
reach you within a week. We were sorry to keep you waiting, but
we would not allow the watch to leave here until it was in good
working order. When the watch arrives, will you please wire us.

X | lax tax axe fix mix oxen exit exact excel boxed expire exile sixth

They expected the experts to examine the texts with extreme care.
I explained that the extra box of index cards was on the sixth shelf.

The six jars that were exported from Mexico have just arrived.
I have examined them with extreme care and find them to be in
excellent condition. So far as I can see, no flaws exist, and the
texture of the clay is exactly as you described it in your exciting
letter. Of course, we cannot fix a price at this time, but an
examination will tell us what we may expect from the next shipment.

EXERCISE 50

s2s s2s k8k k8k s2s s2s k8k k8k s22 k88 s2 k8 s2 k8 s2k8 k82s
Give me the 22 sets. I have only 28. Do you have only 82 more?
d3d d3d j7j j7j d3d d3d j7j j7j d33 j77 d3 j7 d3 j7 d3j7 d37j
See the 77 boys; there are 37 others. I spoke to 73 of them.
f4f f4f 191 191 f4f f4f 191 191 f44 199 f4 19 f4 19 f419 f491
I sold 44 pencils and 99 pens. Tell him to save only 194 for me.

EXERCISE 51

We have received your letter of April 18 and have made a
change in our records to indicate your change of address from
728 Broadway to 194 South 34 Street. The 37 copies of our 29-page
catalog will be sent before May 3 and you should have them in
time for your sale on May 14. May I remind you that we have not
yet received your check for $278 to cover our invoice No. G1742.
This order for 19 cabinets and 32 benches was shipped to you on
March 9 with the understanding that we would receive payment in
thirty days.

EXERCISE 52

f5f f5f j6j j6j f5f j6j f55f j66j f5j6 f5 j6 f5j6 56 j65 f56j
We bought 56 plates, but needed 66. Do you have 5 more to send?
;0; ;0; f4f f4f ;0; ;0; f4f ;0; f4f ;0; 4f 0; 4f0; 4f0; 40;4
The 400 books came today. I expected 440; find the other 40.
s2s d3d f4f f5f ;0; 191 k8k j7j j6j s2 d3 f4 f5 j6 j7 k8 19 ;0
12 123 1234 12345 123456 1234567 12345678 123456789 1234567890

PARAGRAPH STRESSING NUMBER CONTROL

Your letter of June 26 did not receive my attention until 56
today because I left my office on June 9 and did not return until 120
July 31. However, your order will now have immediate attention 182
and should reach you no later than August 7. As I told you, our 245
Price List No. 591 is complete and you can order from it at your 308
convenience. An order for 480 books was sent on the morning of 370
May 25 to the following address: H. Hahn, 371 North 28 Street, 432
New York 31, N. Y. We were happy to be of assistance. 485

Lesson 32

ALPHABET DRILLS (Continued)

S see say she sir sale same sell send sent show size sold some soon

I last saw the scissors when his sister used them for the dresses. Since a small deposit is necessary, I shall certainly send it soon.

Several months ago, we published a series of science books for use in the high schools of our state. These books were designed to stimulate strong interest among students, and the messages sent us assure us that our purpose enjoys enthusiastic success. Since teachers and students have expressed satisfaction with this series, we should like to send some to you for your inspection. May we send them at our expense?

T the too try two take than then them time thank their today truly these

The contract stipulated that we must transport our goods by fast freight. As I told you yesterday, it is essential that you act immediately on it.

Thank you for extending to us the opportunity to test the interesting device for which you recently received a patent. As we stipulated in the last letter that we sent you, we are interested in anything that we think will better the quality of our product, and the tests conducted by our experts indicate that your invention is just exactly what we need. However, the situation in our plant at the present time does not permit the installation of test equipment, but we will get in touch with you at a future date.

U use urge until upon under union upper upset utter undo used unless

You should urge your students to study more thoughtfully than usual. Unless you do your duty, you cannot be assured a successful future.

Your inquiry about the United Hotel is very much valued, and it is our pleasure to rush the literature you requested. During the past four years, we have built up a reputation for the utmost in quality service, and it is no surprise that we have become the most popular resort in the county.

Lesson 26

ALPHABET DRILLS

A | are add ago all and ask any ace able also about above after
An aged man sat wearily beneath an oak and ate a sandwich.
He said that he called Alice to say that the mail was late.

Our annual hardware catalog was sent by mail today and should reach you in a day or two. We also sent our latest price list to replace the one you already had. All items in the catalog can be purchased at any local hardware dealer in Albany, and each purchase carries a two-year guarantee that assures your satisfaction.

B | bed boy buy box beg bit back best banks brings being billing
The baby sobbed when the rubber ball tumbled from the crib.
A number of boys climbed nimbly aboard the boat in the harbor.

You will probably be glad to know that our library has now established a special book section for the boys in your biology and botany club. The books that we have obtained are the best available on the subject, and I believe that the members of the club will derive great benefit from their use. Please place a notice on your bulletin board about our library so that the boys may begin borrowing books immediately.

C | can car cut cub call city came cold card come care copy case
He crawled into a black cave to escape from the coming storm.
A circus camped in the vacant lot near the civil court building.

In accordance with the contract which you recently signed with our company, you accepted our direct-mail service with the understanding that we could expect a check from you each month. It is now three months since we received your last check. Under the circumstances, you can certainly appreciate the fact that we cannot continue to give service until you have paid the accrued balance of your account. I will appreciate it very much if you would place a check in the mail at once and send it to me.

48

Lesson 31

ALPHABET DRILLS (*Continued*)

P — pal pay put page paid past place price please praise policy powerful

People opposed the plan to publish the report in the newspapers.
Speak to the proper person about putting in your application.

Your subscription to our paper has now been properly posted
and your papers should reach you promptly from now on. Most people
who are particularly interested in all phases of sports will probably
be happy to learn that we propose to expand our popular photography
pages in the near future. Every important sporting event will be
photographed by our reporters, and the captions under each picture
will tell the complete story.

Q — quit quip quill queer queen quite quiet quick quota quote quart

I had acquired the queer quartz ring at the quaint antique shop.
As the queen quizzed the quaking boy, she quite suddenly smiled.

It has been quite a long time since you inquired about our
antique furniture and I am writing to request that you come in
quickly to see our stock. The quality of our antiques has never
been equaled in Quincy, and some of our merchandise is so quaint
that I am sure you will be quick to see its worth. The prices
we quote qualify us to say that we can meet your requirements at
the lowest cost available in Quincy.

R — rid rate read roll rude ring reach right remain round really

At our regular Friday party, we prepared a report for the board.
His reply referred to the bravery of the hero during the storm.

We are returning the radio that you recently forwarded to us for
repair. Unfortunately, the parts that require replacement are no
longer being manufactured, and we are therefore unable to put this
radio in working order for you. We are sorry that we cannot provide
our regular service to you, and we regret that it is necessary to
return the radio in the same condition in which it was received. We
hope we can be of better service to you in the near future.

53

Lesson 27

ALPHABET DRILLS (*Continued*)

D | do day due did date dear does down deal done deals doubt doing

The lady used a garden spade to dig a deep ditch near the door.
A hundred bridges were damaged by the flood that deluged the land.

    I had hoped that I would hear from you regarding the details of the advertising program I drew up on Wednesday. You seemed so delighted with the ideas I mentioned, that I expected some word from you in a day or two. Did the Board of Directors decide against our dividend plan that would double your advertising dollar?

E | end ear egg envy earth east each earn equal edit eight exits

We saw the seven men enter the mine before we heard the explosion.
They met on the street every evening to speak of the day's events.

    Our concern is eager to establish a permanent site in your section, and we therefore expect to send a representative to see you next week. We will need at least three hundred acres for our plant and the homes of our employees. We prefer to have this property near the river. The final decision, however, will depend on what our agent tells us after he speaks with you. Any help you may be able to give him will be very much appreciated.

F | far few for fact fair feel file find from full fine first finest

Four or five men from the office staff offered to find a gift for her.
If you finish the job before the first of May, do not fail to tell me.

    Our firm was founded fifty years ago for the benefit of the families in our fine city. Our belief has always been that very few men are fortunate enough to face the financial difficulties that often follow a long illness and we therefore offer an effective insurance plan to offset a loss of income. If you are fearful for the welfare of your family in times of illness, then call at our office and let our staff give you information about a plan you can well afford.

Lesson 30

ALPHABET DRILLS (Continued)

M | most more miss must much music myself money month made many mile

Make some attempt to measure the minimum mileage we must now go.
The meeting of the alumni ended at midnight, but many members stayed.

March is the month when most homeowners make up their minds to do something about the problem of home repairs. If your home is now in need of repairs, remember to communicate with us because we can manage them with maximum efficiency at minimum cost. If you will mail the enclosed information card immediately, we will make arrangements for our men to come to your home to give you a complete estimate.

N | now not new name near need next nice note never notice nature number

It began to rain during the ninth inning, but no one wanted to leave.
The manufacturer announced his intention to conduct a national sale.

A number of men from your company have recently written to ask us for information concerning our new group insurance plan. I am now writing to inquire if we cannot outline a plan wherein one of our agents can attend a meeting conducted in the recreation room in your plant. I know that the entire group of men will benefit from such a general meeting and it will certainly be to their advantage to hear the answers to the questions raised by the individuals in the group.

O | off out over open only often once ours other obey order obliged

To honor our town's hero, the school board voted to close school.
The police worked overtime to locate the one who stole the opals.

I am sorry to inform you that the policy of our company does not allow me to forward the report you ordered now. However, in order to be as helpful as possible, I am enclosing a report of our study recently conducted in one of the major counties; I hope that it will prove of some worth to you in your work. If you would consider coming to my office sometime this month, I might possibly be in a position to offer more information to you.

Lesson 28

G | got gave give girl glad gone good great guess game goes grades

During the spring, he organized a big storage company in Georgia.
The guard saw the garbage barge as it struggled against the tide.

We are going to begin our big luggage sale on Monday. Every
single piece of baggage will be offered at bargain prices and we
suggest that you take advantage of the huge savings that we are
making available. Bring your wife along so that she may see the
gorgeous alligator bags that we also stock. You will both agree
that we are giving the best goods that can be bought for low prices.

H | he his him has had hit hot her how hope hard hear here high home

He thought he should tell the truth although he feared punishment.
The hero marched through the whole town with his head held high.

Have you had a chance to check the rough draft of the pamphlet
which I sent to you on the fourth of March? This pamphlet, which
gives the history of photography, has been ready for the publishers
for almost a month, and we wish to go ahead with the printing shortly.
Will you therefore read it thoroughly and let me have whatever comments
you wish to make about its worth. I shall appreciate your help.

I | in it is if irk into idea item iced iota infer indeed include illness

Learning to type is an art which requires patience and practice.
In a little while, I will again insist that the girl give a decision.

This is in reply to your inquiry about Miss Irene Wilis. Miss
Wilis was hired by our institute five years ago and since that time
has proved highly efficient and reliable in her duties. Her ability
as a statistical typist made her services invaluable and she displayed
genuine initiative in handling the minute details involved in her job.
I think you will find her well qualified for the position in your firm.

Lesson 29

J | jar job just July jail jamb jeer jerk jolt jury jump jilt join jacks

The juggler was injured just before the July job at the Bijou.
The jeweler jumped for joy when the jury gave a judgment in his favor.

In January you joined our Junior Book Club and, judging by your comments, we judge that you are enjoying your membership. This is just to let you know that we have just received a manuscript of jungle stories by B. J. Jorkman that will reach you in June or July. If, however, the subject does not interest you, just jot us a note stating your objection and we will send some other book.

K | key kid keep kept kill kind knee keen king kiss know knife kite

He took the broken knife from the kitchen and kept it in his pocket.
The baker burned his knuckles as he took the cake from the brick oven.

Thank you for the check which reached my desk today. I am very glad to know that you think highly of our books. We expect to make up your order at once and ship it by truck before the end of the week. I spoke to Mr. Baker about the book for which you have asked, and he thinks that it has not been kept in stock for some time. However, we will keep looking and will make every effort to locate it as quickly as possible.

L | lie law lay leg let life less last loft late learn large leaving

While I played a plaintive lullaby, the ailing child fell asleep.
We collected all the blue flowers that blossomed in the fields.

Following our usual policy, we have mailed you a folder which describes fully the glass bottles that our plant makes. The great skill with which all our able employees do their job has never been excelled, and our label on a product is a sure sign of excellent quality. Look through the folder while you have it before you and place your order for holiday glasses immediately.